THE GREATEST LYNCHING
IN AMERICAN HISTORY

THE GREATEST LYNCHING
IN AMERICAN HISTORY
NEW YORK, 1863

Dr. Samuel W. Mitcham, Jr.

SHOTWELL PUBLISHING
Columbia, South Carolina

THE GREATEST LYNCHING IN AMERICAN HISTORY: NEW YORK 1863

Copyright © 2020 by DR. SAMUEL W. MITCHAM, JR.

Produced in the Republic of South Carolina by

SHOTWELL PUBLISHING, LLC
Post Office Box 2592
Columbia, South Carolina 29202

www.ShotwellPublishing.com

Cover Image: "Rowdy Notions of Emancipation", John Tenniel; London *Punch*, August 8, 1863
Cover Design: Hazel's Dream / Boo Jackson TCB

ISBN: 978-1-947660-26-7

10 9 8 7 6 5 4 3 2 1

AUTHOR'S NOTE

The American South has long held an undeserved reputation as the historical center for lynching in the United States. Although there is a small grain of truth in this characterization (certain Southerners did sometimes take the law into their own hands), the West and North had their fair share as well. Alabama and Mississippi were, in fact, pikers compared to New York City when it comes to lynching. It is an actual historical fact that the greatest mass murder of African Americans in United States' history took place during the New York Draft Riots of July 1863, which were also the greatest riots in American history. This is the story of those riots.

Dr. Samuel W. Mitcham, Jr.

TABLE OF CONTENTS

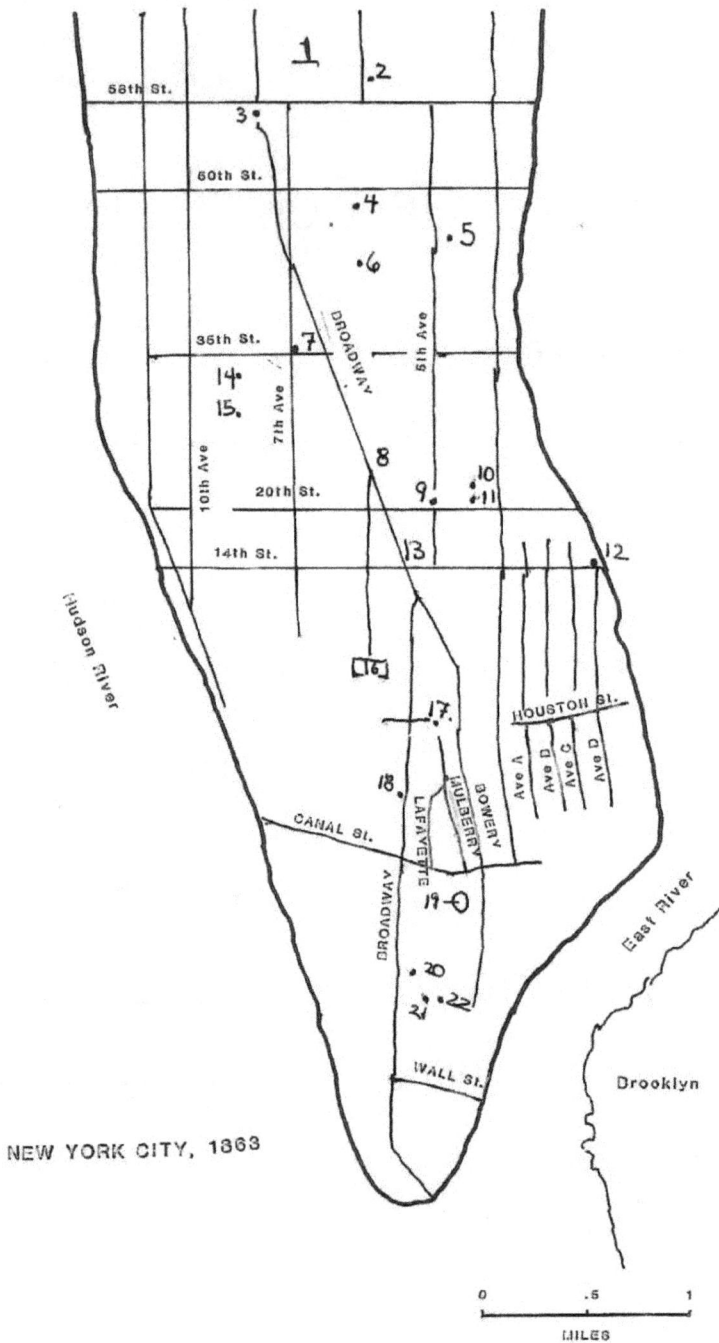

NEW YORK CITY, 1863

58th St.

1

.2

3.

50th St.

.4

.5

.6

35th St.   7

BROADWAY   5th Ave

14.

15.

7th Ave

10th Ave   20th St.   8

9.   10

.11

14th St.   13   12

Hudson River

[16]

17.

HOUSTON St.

18.

CANAL St.

LAFAYETTE   MULBERRY   BOWERY   Ave A   Ave D   Ave C   Ave B

BROADWAY

19-O

East River

.20

21   .22

WALL St.   Brooklyn

0   .5   1

MILES

Map 1

This map shows the major streets only.
Many smaller streets have been omitted for the sake of legibility.

KEY TO MAP I

1. Central Park

2. Central Park Arsenal

3. Black Joke Fire Company

4. Columbia College

5. 9th District Draft Office

6. Colored Orphan Asylum

7. 35th Street Arsenal

8. Madison Square

9. Gramercy Park

10. Union Steam Works

11. State Armory

12. Delameter Iron Works

13. Union Square

14. 20th Precinct Station House

15. Gibbons House

16. Washington Square

17. Police Central

18. St. Nicholas Hotel

19. Five Points

20. City Hall

21. New York Times Building

22. New York Tribune

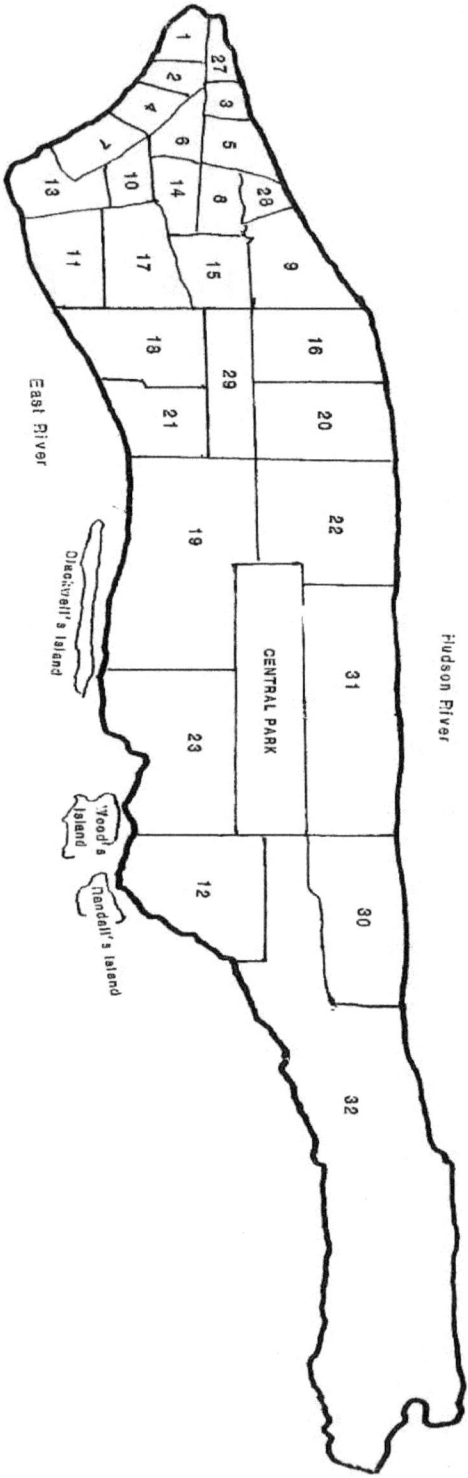

Map 2

The Precincts of New York County, 1863. The 24th, 25th and 26th Precincts had no direct territorial responsibilities and are not shown. The 24th Precinct was responsible for the New York waterfront and headquartered on Police Steamboat No. 1. The 25th Precinct was the Police Central (i.e., General Headquarters) precinct. The 26th Precinct was the City Hall force and was located in the basement of City Hall.

CHAPTER I
THE POWDER KEG

Historic New York was a much different place than the city is today. It was founded by the Dutch in 1609 and christened New Amsterdam. Taken over by the English in 1664, the city was renamed New York, after James, the Duke of York, one of the largest slave traders in history. It was retaken by the Dutch in 1673, when it was renamed "New Orange," but was permanently ceded to the English—along with the entire New Netherland colony—in 1674, in exchange for Suriname.[1]

Largely because of its excellent harbor, New York prospered and, among other things, became a center of slavery and the Trans-Atlantic slave trade. Its people were not only transporters of "black goods" (i.e., people), they were also consumers. By 1703, slavery was a respected institution in the city, more than 42% of all households owned slaves,[2] and it had one of the largest slave populations of any British colony.

But there were problems. In 1712, some of the slaves revolted, killed nine white people and injured six others. The uprising collapsed quickly. Seventy people of African descent were arrested, and 27 were put on trial. Of these, 21 were tried and executed. One was placed on a breaking wheel (i.e., he was tortured to death). The rest were burned to death. Six others reportedly committed suicide before they could be tried.

---

1 Suriname (sometimes spelled Surinam) was a colony and is now a country in northeastern South America.

2 Adele Oltman, "The Hidden History of Slavery in New York," *The Nation*, November 7, 2005.

The colony responded by limiting African American freedom even further. Slaves were not permitted to gather in groups of more than three, they were not allowed to carry firearms, or gamble, and damaging property, conspiring to revolt, or rape were all punishable by death.

These new laws did not prevent further insurrections. In 1741, fires broke out in New York City, including one in the lieutenant governor's home. Subsequent investigation exposed what became known as the Conspiracy of 1741, the Negro Plot of 1741, or the Slave Insurrection of 1741. The guilty or those suspected of being guilty were promptly arrested. More than 200 people were incarcerated, including 20 impoverished whites, and more than 100 people were hanged, exiled, or burned at the stake. The two leaders were gibbetted (i.e., hung in chains in a public display and left to die of exposure, thirst, and starvation). At least 38 slaves and several whites were executed, and 14 Negroes were burned at the stake.[3]

Despite occasional slave revolts, the "Peculiar Institution" continued to thrive in the North. By 1750, there were three times as many slaves in Connecticut as there were in Georgia, and Massachusetts had four times as many as the Peach State.[4] But history was making one of its periodic turns. The Age of Enlightenment (also called the Age of Reason) dawned. Led mainly by philosophers such as Francis Bacon, Rene Descartes, John Locke, Baruch Spinoza, Denis Diderot, Immanuel Kant, Montesquieu, Rousseau, Adam Smith, Voltaire, and Thomas Jefferson, it flooded the world with more enlightened ideas, including manumission and the abolishment of slavery.

This, of course, did not mean white Northerners had any particular love or respect for Negroes. Like Abraham Lincoln, they didn't want white Northerners to have to compete for low-wage jobs. As soon as the labor supply in the North became sufficient to reduce the cost of white labor (which it did through immigration and high birth rates), the New Englanders and New Yorkers began to reduce the number of slaves in their region proportionally. By 1776,

---

3 "Witchhunt in New York: The 1741 Rebellion," https://pbs.org/wgbh/aia/part1/1p286.html; Daniel Horsmanden, "The New York Conspiracy of 1741," in the Gilder Institute of American History. https://gilderlehrman.org/content/ new-york-conspiracy-1741; E. W. R. Ewing, *Northern Rebellion and Southern Secession* (Richmond, Virginia: 1904).

4 "Statistics on Slavery." faculty.weber.edu/kmackay/statistics_on_slavery.html.

Georgia bypassed New York in terms of numbers of black people in bondage, even though it still had more than 10,000 slaves when the American Revolution began. Georgia had around 15,000 chattels.[5]

Pennsylvania enacted a gradual emancipation act in 1780.[6] Five years later, the New York Manumission[7] Society was established with the objective of gradually abolishing slavery within the state's borders. The state legislature passed a progressive abolition law in 1799, with the goal of eliminating slavery by 1827. Rhode Island also passed a manumission law, but it was "very carefully written" to protect the slave trade, which was enriching the state.[8] All the Northern states had enacted anti-slavery legislation by 1830. All the Northern manumission and emancipation laws were designed so that the slaves' owners did not lose money. All the laws had a liberation date. If a slave was born before that date, he would most likely be a slave the rest of his/her life, unless he successfully escaped or was freed by his master. If a slave was born after that date, he would be freed on his 21st birthday—at least theoretically. Master, however, could sell his slaves south before the liberation date. If the law stated that a slave would be liberated on his 21st birthday, for example, the black person could feel pretty confident he would be in a tobacco field in Virginia or a rice paddy in South Carolina when that birthday occurred. There was, as of yet, no moral outrage against slavery in the North. Most of the momentum behind manumission was a desire to protect white labor from cheap African competition.

Even after the slaves were freed, they were not welcomed in the North. This fact is reflected in the declining population of Northern blacks in relation to whites. The censuses from 1790 to 1830 indicate a proportional decline in the

---

5 See Jeffrey R. Hummel, *Emancipating Slaves, Enslaving Free Men* (Chicago: 1996) (hereafter cited as "Hummel").

6 *Ibid*, p. 10.

7 Manumission takes place when owners free their slaves voluntarily. Emancipation is the process of freeing slaves through government action. Emancipation is done gradually and can involve compensation. Abolition is when a government ends slavery completely. It could be done all at once or in increments. No compensation was required.

8 Edgar J. McManus, *Emancipating Slaves, Enslaving Free Men* (Chicago: 1966), p. 168.

free Negro population of New York from 2.13% to 0.57%. Quite a few were kidnapped and sold into slavery elsewhere. There were 33 reported kidnappings of black people in New York City alone in a single year.[9]

Meanwhile, periodic riots occurred in New York City, and some of them had nothing to do with slavery. Others did. It was a turbulent city beset by a corrupt politician machine, immigration, widespread poverty, and a restless population. A partial list of the major riots included the Stamp Act Riot of 1765, the Doctors' Riot of 1788,[10] the Bread Riots of 1807 and 1808, the Election Riot of 1834, the Anti-Abolition Riot of 1834, the Anti-Abolition Riot of 1835, the Flour Riot of 1837, the Astor Place Riots of 1849, and the Police Riot of 1857, which was also known as the Dead Rabbits' Riot or Bread Riot of 1857.

As the Civil War approached in 1860, the population of the city stood at 813,669. It was almost exactly divided between immigrants and native born Americans. There were more than 210,000 Irish immigrants residing in the city and more than 100,000 Germans. The new arrivals were poor and not favorably disposed toward African American men, with whom they were competing for low-wage jobs. (There were fewer than 13,000 blacks living in New York in 1863.) The corporate employers took full advantage of this situation, of course, to keep wages low. Irish, Germans, and Negroes alike generally lived in poverty.

The Irish immigrants in particular lived in incredible penury. Their situation grew even worse after the Lincoln regime provoked Confederate President Jefferson Davis into firing on Fort Sumter on April 12, 1861. New York City's textile industry depended upon cotton from the South, and now that resource was cut off. Many of the city's factories and textile mills were forced to shut down, which threw thousands of low-wage immigrants out of work.[11] (Low wages were better than no wages in those days.) The destitution of the Irish immigrants was especially widespread in the lower (South) side and on the East Side of Manhattan around Five Points and the Bowery. People lived in densely packed slums, often an entire family in a single room. A committee sent to study the problem saw one room, which was 12 x 12 feet, was inhabited by 20 people of all ages and sexes. Some people made a living by collecting dung from the

---

9 *Ibid*, p. 182.

10 This riot occurred after it became known that medical students were robbing graves to obtain cadavers for their studies.

11 Charles River Editors, *The New York Draft Riots of 1863* (Columbia, South Carolina: 2016), n.p. (hereafter cited as "Charles River")

streets. They sold it for $.04 per basket.[12] Many of them didn't even have even a single piece of furniture. The streets were knee-deep in mud, garbage was everywhere, all of the rundown buildings were infected with rats, roaches, and other vermin, the residents dressed in rags (which was all they had), children went barefoot even in the winter, and pigs rooted in the streets. Conditions were worse than even the notoriously bad London slums. These Irish people came to the New World seeking opportunity but found only unemployment, crushing poverty, and misery. Many of them became beggars. Others became alcoholics and drunks. There were plenty of saloons and cheap whiskey here. Thousands of people turned to liquor to relieve the misery that permeated these slums. Others turned to prostitution or crime. On the South Side, the Lower East Side, and along the waterfront, bordellos were everywhere.

So was violence and begging. James McCague tells the story of a little girl who begged for a handout and received a penny from a benefactor. Someone murdered her—for a penny!—and stole it. Her family lived in a cellar with a dirt floor. The girl's mother could not afford to pay for a funeral, so she dug a swallow grave in the cellar and buried her there.[13] This kind of burial was common in the Bowery and Five Points in 1860.

Crime was also widespread. The records show more than 80,000 arrests in 1862—about 10% of the total population—and the extant records are incomplete.[14]

There were also gangs—and a lot of them. They included the Dead Rabbits, the Roach Guards, the Shirt Tails, the Plug Uglies, the Bowery Boys (or Bowery B'hoys), the Chichesters, the Kerryonians, the Buckoos, the Daybreak Boys, the Honeymoon Gang, the Hookers,[15] the Slaughter Housers, the Swamp Angels, the Patsey Conroys, and several others. The members of these gangs would see a major riot as an opportunity not only to vent their frustrations but to loot, pillage, and acquire weapons for further extra-legal activities.

---

12 Adrian Cook, *The Armies of the Streets* (Lexington, Kentucky: 1974), p. 28.

13 James McCague, *The Second Rebellion* (New York: 1968), p. 22.

14 *Ibid*, p. 26.

15 The meaning of words often change over time. The term "hooker" did not begin to refer to a female prostitute until 1863, and it did not become a common expression for prostitute until sometime after that.

Poverty, cheap booze, or just personal inclination turned many of the immigrants to crime. For others, it was the need to belong to a group which accepted them or just shared their values and interests. Crime also represented a kind of employment to which desperate people turned when other types of employment were lacking. The neighborhoods were so bad that the police were afraid to patrol them alone. They usually patrolled in squads of six or more. Even then there were some establishments the police would not enter, even if they were pursuing a suspect who ran into the place. They knew they might well be killed if they did.

The Irish also resented the predominant American prejudice against new immigrants. When jobs were advertised, the advertisement frequently contained the stipulation: "Irish need not apply." Some businesses even displayed signs which proclaimed, "No dogs or Irishmen allowed."

CHAPTER II
THE SPARK

A s incredible as this statement may sound to some modern readers, New York City was largely sympathetic to the South as the Civil War approached. Although the state voted for Lincoln, the city cast its ballots against him by a margin of 2 to 1. When he was nevertheless elected president and South Carolina seceded, there was something akin to panic in the city's business community. One scholar spoke nothing but the truth when he said the road to profits on Wall Street ran through the cotton fields of the South. Samuel F. B. Morse, the highly respected inventor of the telegraph, esteemed attorney Samuel J. Tilden, and famous newspaper editor Horace Greeley, among others, supported the idea of a peaceful separation.

Many immigrants felt the same way. Undoubtedly, many of the Irish opposed the possible emancipation of the slaves because of the competition for low-wage jobs which might result.[16] They therefore hoped the South would win the war. A great many of them were indeed not prepared to die for the "Glorious Union."

The city's corrupt mayor, Democrat Fernando Wood, who was allied with the immigrants, agreed.[17] In a speech to a predominantly German crowd, Wood said the abolitionists "will prosecute it [the war] so long as there is a drop of Southern blood to be shed, provided they are removed from the scene of danger.

---

16   http://www.mrlincolnandnewyork.org/new-york-politics/mr-lincoln-and-new-york-politics/ citing Leslie M. Harris, *In the Shadow of Slavery: African Americans in New York City, 1626-1863* (Chicago: 2003), p. 279.

17 Fernando Wood was born in Philadelphia in 1812. He moved to New York City, became a successful shipping merchant, and joined the corrupt Tammany Hall political machine. He served in Congress (1841-43) and was mayor of New York from 1855 to 1858 and 1860 to 1862. He supported Confederate independence.

They will get Irish and Germans to fill their regiments to 'defend the country' under the idea that they themselves will remain at home, and divide the plunder . . ."[18] He even floated the idea of New York City seceding from both the state and the nation. It would then be able to receive a constant flow of cotton from the South for its textile and garment industries. Nothing came of the idea, however, because war came too soon.

On April 12, 1861, Confederate guns fired on Fort Sumter, South Carolina. Because the South had fired on Old Glory, and not knowing all of the facts, Northern public opinion united behind the Union war effort. They marched off to war to the sound of rousing speeches, cheering crowds, and brass bands. They were going to crush the "traitors," and within 90 days. Surely the war would be over soon . . .

But it wasn't.

* * *

On September 22, 1862, Abraham Lincoln issued the Emancipation Proclamation, declaring the slaves in areas in rebellion free if they did not return to the Union by January 1, 1863. It was an executive order of dubious legality and, as Lincoln himself admitted, was a war measure. It was not particularly well received in the North, especially among the new immigrants. Mired at the bottom of the economic ladder, the Irish were deeply apprehensive that a wave of newly freed blacks would flood New York City and take the low-skill, low-wage jobs which they currently held. They didn't have much, and now they faced the prospect of losing even that. They were not happy.

In March 1863, the Irish ship and dock workers went on strike. They wanted the same wages increased from $2.50 to $3 per 12-hour day—the same pay as ships' carpenters. The corporate fat cats countered by bringing in 200 African American strikebreakers, who were protected by armed guards. The Irish responded by physically attacking the blacks anyway. There were casualties on both sides, although the police broke up the riot before anyone was killed. In the minds of many Irish immigrants, it confirmed the fears engendered by the Emancipation Proclamation. Negroes were already taking low-wage Irish jobs!

---

18 http://www.mrlincolnandnewyork.org/new-york-politics/mayoral-elections/ citing Sidney D. Brummer, *Political History of New York State During the Period of the Civil War*, (Wahroonga: 2015) p. 176

As they contemplated the likelihood of having to watch their families starve, they were angry and afraid. It would not be difficult to work them up into a mindless frenzy.

As 1863 dawned, Northern enthusiasm for the war evaporated under the withering blasts of Confederate muskets, rifles, and cannons. Voluntary Union enlistments slowed to a trickle, and Lincoln's foreign mercenaries were not enough to fill the ranks.[19] Due to his heavy casualties, lack of success, and with the allure and romance of the war dissipating, Lincoln resorted to conscription. The Federal Draft Act passed Congress and was signed into law on March 3.[20]

Although the Confederacy instituted a draft a year earlier, this was the first time the United States did so in its history, and there was strong opposition to it. The draft was denounced as "tyrannical, despotic, [and] unjust . . . an act which has distinguished tyrants the world over, and should never be tolerated by a free people."[21] Certainly many strong Unionists thought it was a violation of their individual rights. Elements of the press hinted that it was not only a right, but a duty, to oppose it.

The most odious feature of the act was that rich people who could pay $300 ($6,069.07 in 2017 money[22]) were exempted from conscription. This was about the equivalent of a year's wages for the average worker. African Americans—who were not considered citizens at the time—were also excused from the draft. The Irish immigrants in general and the striking longshoremen in particular were already angry. Now they faced the prospect of being drafted into the Union Army to, as James Howell Street wrote, "face death to give freedom to Negro slaves whose cousins had taken their jobs."

It was too much.[23]

---

19 During the war, 2,750,000 men served in the Union Army during the war. Of these, 489,200 were foreign mercenaries, including 200,000 Germans, 150,000 Irishmen, 60,000 British and Canadians. The rest came from a dozen other countries. About 800,000 men served in the Confederate Army.

20 E.B. Long, *The Civil War Day by Day* (Garden City, New York: 1971), p. 325.

21 Headley, Joel Tyler. *The Great Riots of New York*. New York: 1873, p. 136

22 Morgan Friedman Inflation Calculator.

23 James Howell Street, *The Civil War* (New York, 1953), p. 90.

Meanwhile, in May 1863, despite being outnumbered more than 2 to 1, Robert E. Lee's Army of Northern Virginia crushed the Union Army of the Potomac at Chancellorsville. It invaded the North in June. Shocked and panicky, the Lincoln regime called up every military unit it could get its hands on. This included almost the entire New York Militia/National Guard,[24] including the 17 regiments in New York City. In the meantime, the U.S. War Department announced that the draft would commence on July 11. No request was made for police protection for the enrollment officers, nor for the offices where the draft would take place. The only guard details available were provided by the Invalid Corps: 500 crippled soldiers under the command of Colonel Ruggles.[25] They were unquestionably brave and loyal men, but they were also physically unfit for field service and would prove totally unable to deal with large-scale rioting.

Only New York Governor Horatio Seymour (a Democrat) sensed trouble.[26] He requested that Washington postpone the draft. But the Lincoln administration was complacent and ignored his request. The draft went forward as scheduled.

There were, in my view, five major factors in the riot:

1) A Cause. The Draft provided this.

2) A Criminal Nucleus. The gangs provided this.

3) Weak Repressive Forces. General Lee and President Lincoln were responsible for this.

4) Good weather. It was summer, and the weather was good for rioting. God provided this.

---

24 On April 23, 1862, all New York militia units were redesignated National Guard units; however, many people continued to refer to them as militia. In this book, the two terms will be used interchangeably.

25 Ruggles was a former staff officer of Major General John Pope. Pope led the Army of Virginia until it was smashed by General Lee in the Second Battle of Manassas (August 1862). Pope was then sent into professional exile and so, apparently, was Ruggles.

26 Horatio Seymour was born in Pompey, New York, in 1810. He had a long political career, which included a term as mayor of Utica (1842-43) and in the New York State Assembly (1843-45). He also managed his family's business interests, including real estate, banks, railroads, mines, and other enterprises. He was the Democratic gubernatorial nominee in 1850 but narrowly lost the election. He was elected governor in 1852, was defeated for reelection by only 309 votes in 1854, but ran again in 1862 and was elected.

Mayor Fernando Wood

Governor Horatio Seymour.

11

5) A False Sense of Security Among the Leadership and the General Public.

The draft began at 9 a.m. on Saturday, July 11, beginning in the 9th and 11th Districts. Captain Joel T. Erhardt, the provost marshal in the 9th District, tried to hold a draft at the corner of Broadway and Liberty Street, near where a work crew was demolishing a building. One man with an iron bar in his hand approached the captain, with the obvious intention of murdering him. Fortunately for Erhardt, he had a pistol, which he drew and aimed at the man's chest. Seeing the officer meant business, the worker dropped the bar.

Erhardt resumed the draft but, sometime later, the man returned and attacked Erhardt. The enrollment officer managed to beat him off and pull his pistol again, but the other workmen supported the attacker and surrounded the captain. Erhardt sent three messengers to his superior, Colonel Robert Nugent,[27] begging for help, but he sent none. The standoff lasted three hours before the workers left. No one was arrested.[28] Erhardt resumed his draft. According to William O. Stoddard, a private secretary of Abraham Lincoln, many of those selected were well known to the police.[29]

Another draft took place at 677 3rd Avenue, near 46th Street. Captain Charles E. Jenkins of the Provost Marshal's Office directed proceedings, which were professional and business-like. The operation was observed by a gloomy and sullen crowd. By 6 p.m., 1,236 names were drawn. Captain Jenkins announced that only 264 more men were needed to fulfill the district's quota, and the draft would resume on Monday, July 13. The unhappy crowd slowly dispersed.

In those days, saloons and bars were open on Sunday. Unhappy Irishmen gathered at their favorite watering holes and discussed the day's events over cheap ale and bad whiskey—something they often did. But today was different. This time, they were prepared to act.

---

27 Robert Nugent was the provost marshal for the Southern District of New York, including New York City and Long Island. Born in Ireland in 1824, he joined the 69th New York Militia Regiment prior to the war. In 1861, he was commissioned captain in the Regular Army and assisted in recruiting the Irish Brigade. He was given command of the 69th, which was reconstituted as an infantry regiment. He led it well in the Battles of Seven Pines and the Seven Days Campaign (including the Battles of Gaines Mill, Savage Station, Frazer's Farm, and Malvern Hill). He was shot in the stomach at Fredericksburg.

28 Headley, pp. 147-48.

29 William O. Stoddard, *Volcano Under the City* (New York: 1887), p. 21.

July 12 was a day of fermentation and suppressed excitement. There were no external signs of the approaching disorder. There were two or three fires, but nobody connected them to the draft. They did attract more than the usual crowds, and they were more disorderly than usual, but no one thought much about it. The New York *Tribune* reported that everything had gone quietly. New York City Police Superintendent John Kennedy did take the precaution of sending Sergeant Van Orden and 15 policemen to the arsenal at 35th Street and 7th Avenue, even though no one had asked him to do so. As night fell on July 12, complacency prevailed among the military, civilian, and police leadership in New York City.

CHAPTER III
THE LEADERSHIP

A nd to whom would fall the task of dealing with the deadliest riot in American history?

The superintendent of police was John A. Kennedy, who had a long history of working with immigrants and protecting them against swindlers. His father was an Irish immigrant who became a school teacher in Baltimore, where Kennedy was born in 1803. John moved to New York City, went into business with his brother, and became commissioner of emigration in 1849. He became police superintendent in 1860.

Kennedy was also a Democrat, although he was not a stooge of the party's corrupt Tammany Hall political machine, which nevertheless exercised considerable control over the police.

The New York police force was riddled with corruption, political factionalism, and divided loyalties. Mayor Fernando Wood often made police appointments based on favoritism rather than merit, sold offices, took bribes, received kickbacks from contractors, and did favors for the gangs, who supported him with votes and worked for his reelection. In 1857, to acquire power over the police and to mitigate the corruption of Mayor Wood, the New York state legislature created the Metropolitan Board of Police Commissioners and abolished the Municipal Police Department. The new board was given control over the police in the counties of New York (which included Manhattan and Brooklyn), Kings, Westchester, and Richmond. Initially, the board chairman was Frederick Augustus Tallmadge, a famous abolitionist and noted reformer.

The new commission ordered Wood to disband the Municipal Police and turn its men and property over to the Metropolitans. Wood refused to do so and took the matter to court, where he lost. Even then, Wood refused to comply. A warrant was issued for his arrest, and the police department split into two armed factions. This led to the Police Riot of 1857—an indecisive battle between two police factions (see below). The gangs loved it. They went on a crime spree. Municipal (pro-Wood) police often interfered with Metropolitans when they attempted to arrest gang members. Even when a ganger was incarcerated, the Municipals often released him on his own recognizance.

The legal battle continued for some time. The civil courts ruled that the governor had no legal right to interfere in mayoral appointments, but in the fall of 1857, the Court of Appeals sustained the Metropolitans.

Eventually, the Republican governor, John King, ordered Wood to leave his office and surrender. Wood refused. King restored order by sending in the 7th New York State Militia Regiment (commanded by Major General Charles W. Sandford), which surrounded City Hall. Seeing his position was hopeless, Wood gave himself up but was out on bail within an hour. In time, the Republicans prevailed and Wood agreed to disband the Municipal Police. He was never brought to trial, but that may have been part of a deal.

The Police Riot, 1857: Municipals vs. Metropolitians.

Six years later, in 1863, the police were still divided politically. Kennedy was a Democrat and Thomas C. Acton, the President of the Metropolitan Board of Police Commissioners, was a staunch Republican who wholeheartedly supported Lincoln's war effort. He was also a broker by trade with little experience in law enforcement.

Another factor made certain observers question the policeman's loyalty. Many if not most of the men wearing the badges were Irish Catholics. The rioters were also Irish Catholics. Neither group supported Mr. Lincoln's War. The only difference between the police and the rioters, in fact, was their attitude toward law and order. Some people wondered if they would have the will to be effective against the mob. They need not have concerned themselves. The police would use their billy clubs and bust heads with great enthusiasm.

In 1862, Wood was defeated for reelection by George Opdyke, a Republican. He was an affable businessman and an honest person but was nervous and not particularly effective during a crisis. He would only serve one term.

The senior military officer in New York was Major General John E. Wool, the commander of the Department of the East. Born in Newburgh in 1784, he joined the army as an infantry captain when the War of 1812 broke out and distinguished himself in combat against the British. Remaining in the army after the war, he became a brigadier general in 1841 and won fresh laurels and a brevet promotion to major general during the Mexican War. He participated in the Peninsula Campaign of 1862, where he captured Norfolk, Virginia. Abraham Lincoln reportedly witnessed this event personally and promoted Wool to major general, Regular Army. Wool briefly commanded the VIII Corps before the president decided he had reached an age where he should have a less demanding assignment. Wool assumed command of the Department of the East on January 3, 1863.

Although unquestionably a hero of the first order and a man to be admired, Wool was 79 years old in 1863 and unable to personally direct troops. He was also totally out of place in a domestic riot situation. He would not be an effective leader during the riots.

Major General Charles Sandford commanded the New York Militia, which did not amount to much on July 13. Most of it was in Pennsylvania or in Maryland, pursuing Lee's army, which had been defeated at Gettysburg (July 1-3). Sandford was an old soldier. Born in Newark, New Jersey, in 1796, he became a lawyer and entered the New York Militia as an artillery private around 1814. He became a brigadier general and militia brigade commander in 1834, was promoted to major general and division commander in 1839, and was the state's senior militia officer for the next 29 years. He was slow, fond of military

Mayor Opdyke

New York City Police Superintendent
John A. Kennedy

Major General Charles W. Sandford

Major General John Wool

pomp and ceremony, and at first refused to believe a major disturbance was in progress. He would be a totally ineffective commander in 1863.

Brevet Brigadier General Harvey E. Brown, the commander of Fort Hamilton and the garrison of New York harbor, was an altogether different kind of animal than Sandford. Born in Bridgetown (now part of Rahway), New Jersey, in 1795, he graduated from West Point in 1818 and was commissioned in the artillery. Between garrison assignments, he fought in the Black Hawk War, the 2nd Seminole War (where he earned a brevet to major) and the Mexican War (where he was brevetted lieutenant colonel and colonel), and the 3rd Seminole War. He was military commander of the Washington, D.C., defenses from January until May 1861, when he was named commander of the 5th Artillery Regiment. Sent to Florida, he successfully defended Fort Pickens and Santa Rosa Island from Confederate attacks in November 1861. He was brevetted brigadier general in April 1862, the same month he was appointed commander of New York Harbor. Brown was a combat veteran, a real leader, and became de facto commander of the military forces in Manhattan during draft week.

* * *

We can see from this brief description that the leaders of the anti-mob forces were a diverse group and varied widely in terms of competence, energy, experience, and reaction time to emergency situations. Some of them made mistakes during the crisis; however, their performance was better than anyone had any right to expect.

* * *

So what about the other side?

No anti-Lincoln or anti-administration leader of any standing advocated rioting or anarchy. There was never a Gangland High Command. From the beginning, the absence of proper organization and the almost total lack of credible leadership proved that the riot was largely spontaneous and not a plot of some sort. There were leaders, however; we just don't know much about them. They were disgruntled strikers who were replaced or fired from their jobs. They were family men who had jobs but were drafted into the army, who were now supposed take a severe reduction in pay to go to Virginia or South Carolina and fight men they did not hate, for the benefit of men they did hate, while their families had to fend for themselves in America's worst slums. They were gang leaders who did not care a rip about the reasons for the war or much else but were glad of this opportunity to plunder and rob. They were men who worked on the wharves, in foundries, in shipyards, in factories, printing houses, and scores of other places, working 12 and 14-hour days, trading time they could never recover for a pittance—frustrated men, who watched their wives dress in rags and grow old, mired in poverty and misery, while things never got better. They were men who fled the Potato Famine in Ireland, only to end up in decaying and vermin-infested tenements in the Land of the Free. They were men who wanted a better life for their children but saw no chance of securing a better future for them. They were men who the American dream had passed by—or turned into a nightmare. They were men who watched helplessly as their offspring went down the same path as they had because they had no other options. They were angry men—men who were ready to lash out at the first opportunity, often without focus or reason. They were determined men, even if they only had the vaguest idea what they were determined about. They were men who realized they now had a golden opportunity to vent their hatred and frustrations on the city, especially on the wealthy or well-to-do, and they intended to take full advantage of this fact. They were men whom their friends and neighbors—who were materially no better off than they—were willing to follow. They were men who were willing to die if necessary, because sometimes death itself is a relief. Oh, yes, they had leaders. And on July 13, they struck.

CHAPTER IV
THE FIRST MORNING (MONDAY, JULY 13)
THE BATTLE OF THE 3RD AVENUE DRAFT OFFICE

On the morning of July 13, groups of men and women began to assemble in the western part of New York City at an alarming rate. (Women would play a prominent role in these riots.) Dissidents—many of whom were gang members—visited factories and workshops and asked the workers to join them. Now was the time to demonstrate against the draft, they declared. If the foremen or proprietors objected, they were threatened with the destruction of their property. Apparently, these threats were always sufficient. The businesses closed and the workers took to the streets.

Early that morning, the engineer in charge of the Croton Reservoir in Central Park found that only half his normal work force showed up. Some feared violence and went home, but they were a minority. Most joined the mob. Police received reports that some of the street contractors' men in the 19th Ward were not working. Superintendent Kennedy became concerned. He did not like the way the storm clouds were gathering. He was also a man of limited resources. He had a total strength of 2,400 policemen, but only 1,620 were patrolmen and half of them were off duty. Even so, he reasoned, if a riot occurred, one of the mob's primary goals would be to obtain weapons, so he sent 50 men to the 7th Avenue Arsenal. At 8:35 a.m. he sent telegrams to the 17th, 18th, and 21st Precincts, ordering each of them to send 10 men and a sergeant to 677 3rd Avenue and to report to Captain Galen T. Porter for duty. Porter, the commander of the 19th Precinct, was in charge of protecting the Enrollment Office at 677 3rd Avenue.

Fifteen minutes later, Kennedy ordered the 29th Precinct to send 10 men under a competent sergeant to protect the draft officials at 1190 Broadway. Five minutes before 9 a.m., he instructed the 16th and 20th Precincts to send their reserves to the 7th Avenue Arsenal immediately. But at 9 a.m., it appeared these precautions were unnecessary. Draft officials walked through gloomy crowds to their duty stations and were not molested.

About 9 a.m., tough characters boarded the street cars on both 2nd and 3rd Avenues above 65th Street and ordered the drivers to stop running their cars and not to attempt further trips—or else. The drivers did as they were told. At the same time, the telegraph wires near the 3rd Avenue Enrollment Office were cut. This was the first act suggesting any forethought on the part of the mob leaders. Stoddard later stated that the mob was not made up of local people but "contained a full proportion of rough and lawless characters."[30] There was excitement in the air. All of the saloons in the vicinity were doing a brisk business, despite the early hour.

At 9 a.m., Superintendent Kennedy ordered all police precincts in New York and Brooklyn to call in their reserve platoons and hold them in the station houses until further orders. It would take some time to execute this order, even without a riot.

In 1863, the New York City Police had a better communications system than any other law enforcement agency in the world. All 32 precincts were in telegraphic communication with Police Central at 300 Mulberry Street. The Superintendent of the Police Telegraph System, James Crowley, left his home in Yorkville that morning and was on his way to work around 9 a.m. when he saw a crowd and downed telegraph wires, including the special police wires. He immediately grasped the situation and, with considerable courage, gathered all the wires and grounded them to a lamp post, so as to insure their continued operations. Drunken rioters approached, threatened him, and demanded to know what he was doing. "Only getting the wires out of your way, boys," he calmly replied. No doubt about it—James Crowley was cool. The drunks accepted his explanation, and he was not harmed. As soon as he was finished, Crowley scurried to the 21st Precinct station house (on 35th Street) and telegraphed Central Office that a mob was forming. This was the first solid information the police had as to the true nature of the situation.[31] Between 5,000 and 6,000 telegrams would be sent over police wires from Monday through Thursday, despite interference from the rioters. Unfortunately for history, the vast majority of these communications were destroyed by the police department, instead of being placed in archives.

---

30 Stoddard, p. 34.

31 Stoddard, pp. 34-35.

Captain Porter was at the 21st Precinct station house and spoke with Crowley. He already had a squad at the 3rd Avenue Enrollment Office. He reinforced to a total of 60 men.

About 9:30 a.m., Superintendent Kennedy could stand it no longer. He left headquarters to investigate the situation personally. He went unescorted in a buggy, first to the 35th Street Arsenal, then to a point near the 3rd Avenue Enrollment Office. He left his buggy and driver there and proceeded on foot. It was a near-fatal mistake. He was in civilian clothes, but one of the rioters (a former policeman) recognized him, shouted to his comrades, and attacked him.

About six of Kennedy's men were nearby and saw he was in trouble. They drew their pistols and pulled their locust wood billy clubs to try to rescue him but were quickly overwhelmed by the mob. The Superintendent was grabbed and pushed six feet down the graded street into a vacant lot. The mob was on him instantly and beat him to a pulp, stabbed him multiple times, and tried to drown him in a mud puddle. By making a supreme effort, he got to his feet and dashed for a pond, which he reached, and waded to the middle of it. The rioters did not want to get wet, so they went to the other side of the pond to wait for him to come out. Luckily, the Superintendent saw Mr. John Eagan, a minor Tammany Hall official and an influential local citizen. "John Eagan!" he cried, "come here and save my life!" Eagan did, although Kennedy was so badly beaten that he did not recognize him. Eagan and a few policemen plopped Kennedy in the back of a passing feed wagon, which took him to Police HQ.

Thomas Acton, meanwhile, went to Police Central. He saw Kennedy when they brought him in, but he was so battered that Acton also did not recognize him. Thinking he was a drunken rioter, he ordered the attending officer to lock him up. Acton was soon corrected, and Kennedy—who was in critical condition—was taken to a surgeon. One report stated he was stabbed 70 times. It would be weeks before he was able to return to duty. He was, in fact, lucky to be alive.

Acton now took over the police department. He was a man of nervous temperament and little experience in law enforcement, but he behaved coolly and correctly throughout the crisis. Given his background, one can only be amazed at how well he performed. His views on how to handle a mob paralleled those of Napoleon I, who once said, "Give them a taste of grape!" (i.e., fire on the mob with cannons and at close range). Acton ordered the police reserves to concentrate at Police Headquarters (on Mulberry Street, near Broadway), from whence he could dispatch forces wherever they were needed.

Police Central Headquarters, 300 Mulberry Street.

The more intelligent members of the mob realized the telegraph wires were vital to the police response. They cut down the wires on 3rd Avenue, severing communications to and from the precincts at Fort Washington, Manhattanville, Harlem, Yorkville, Bloomingdale, and the 19th Precinct. Later, they cut down the poles on 1st Avenue, 22nd Street, and 9th Avenue.[32] Meanwhile, the mob armed itself with every conceivable weapon, including sticks, clubs, iron bars, knives, axes, hatchets, and guns. They pushed toward Central Park, gaining recruits with every block they marched.

The rioters rallied in a vacant lot near the park and then broke into two major bodies, moving down 5th and 6th Avenue until they reached 46th and 47th Street, when they turned east and headed toward 677 3rd Avenue, tearing down telegraph poles along the way. They crossed the Harlem & New Haven Railroad track, and about 500 of them headed toward the building where the draft was being conducted. They were led by the volunteer fire fighters of Engine Company 33. Their captain and other men of the "Black Joke" company[33] were drafted, and

---

32 Headley, pp. 158-59.

33 Black Joke was the name of their fire engine.

they intended to tear up the Enrollment Office, smash the draft wheel, destroy all of the papers (so no one could tell they were drafted), and burn the building to the ground. The police detachment guarding the office did not resist—it would have been both futile and quite likely fatal. As the draft officers fled out the back, the mob stormed into the office, smashed the furniture, and set the building on fire.

Just before 10:30 a.m., a detachment of about 50 men from the Invalid Corps approached the Enrollment Office. They were too late. They were attacked by the mob, which hurled rocks and paving stones into their ranks. The shocked soldiers fired warning shots over their heads, but one rank fired into the mob, killing or wounding several people. This infuriated the rioters, who attacked the soldiers before they could reload, took their muskets away from them, and beat them severely. Most of the Invalids were just bruised, but two of them were beaten to death. The bluecoats fled but were pursued by the mob, which chased them for 10 blocks. One was followed to a ledge overlooking the river, where he was caught. The mob threw him off the ledge and killed him.

Police Central, in the meantime, ordered the reserve sections of 11 different precincts to the scene of the riot. Unfortunately, they all arrived at different times, and the mob defeated each detachment one at a time.

Sergeant Robert A. "Fighting Mac" McCredie of the 15th Precinct led one group of 14 officers from 28th Street to 43rd Street and 3rd Avenue, where he joined 30 other policemen from other precincts. They charged the mob and pushed it back to 46th Street, but there the rioters rallied, turned on the cops, and routed them. Only five of McCredie's men were not wounded in the fighting. Officer William H. Travis suffered a broken jaw, his teeth were knocked out, he was stripped naked, and left for dead. Officer Bennett was more fortunate: the mob allowed him to keep his drawers. Officer Phillips was clubbed and then stabbed twice, in the ear and the arm, by a woman. He was rescued by a stranger who threatened to kill anyone who injured Phillips further. Officer Kiernan was struck by four different stones and a hay-bale rung, and he fell insensible to the pavement. The mob would have murdered him had Mrs. Eagan not thrown herself over his body and cried: "For God's sake do not kill him!" The mob passed them by.[34] Sergeant McCredie himself was also lucky. Running for his life, he entered the home of a young German woman, who had no sympathy for the rabble. She hid the sergeant between two mattresses just before the mob broke in. She coolly told the rioters that McCredie had just escaped via the rear of the house. They believed her and took off in pursuit.

---

34 Headley, p. 164. Mrs. Eagan was the wife of John Eagan, the man who saved Superintendent Kennedy's life.

27

Other wings of the crowd were more interested in looting. The Croton Cottage restaurant on 5th Avenue was looted, as was the Palace Park House, a hotel on 40th Street. There the hoodlums confiscated champagne, rum, gin, assorted other adult beverages, and 1,700 cigars.[35] Other ruffians went into Samuel Crook's saloon on Chatman Street and beat the black waiters who worked there.

Meanwhile, 677 3rd Avenue went up in flames. The upper part of this building were private residences, but the mob thought the officers must have fled there. They pounded it with rocks and brickbats. Joel Tyler Headley, who witnessed the riot, recalled "Deputy Provost Marshal Edward S. Vanderpoel, who had mingled in the crowd, fearing for the lives of the women and children, boldly stepped to the front and tried to appease the mob, telling them the papers were all destroyed, and begged them to fall back, and let others help the inmates of the building . . . The reply was a heavy blow in the face. Vanderpoel shoved the man who gave it aside, when he was assailed with a shower of blows and curses. Fearing for his life, he broke through the crowd, and hastened to the stop where the police were standing, wholly powerless in the midst of this vast, excited throng."

A little after 11 a.m., Captain Porter sent a message from the 19th Precinct to Police Central, stating that the marshal's office on 3rd Avenue was lost and burning down.

"In the meanwhile," Headley recalled, "the flames, unarrested, made rapid way, and communicating to the adjoining building, set it on fire. The volumes of smoke, rolling heavenward, and the crackling and roaring of the flames, seemed to awe the mob . . ."[36]

The fire department responded, but the mob killed their horses and destroyed their engines. They also cut the telegraph wires to prevent anyone from signaling for help. Generally speaking, the volunteer firemen were sympathetic for the rioters. Many of them went home even before the horses were done in.

About 12:25 p.m., Chief Engineer John Decker of the Fire Department spoke to the mob. He told them that they accomplished their purpose, and the draft office was destroyed. The fire was spreading to more and more buildings. He succeeded momentarily, but as he brought up his fire engines, other rioters attacked them from the rear, drove off the firemen, and captured the fire engines. They did not damage the machinery, however.

---

35 Cook, p. 65.

36 Headley, p. 154.

Shortly after, Decker did convince the mob to let the firemen do their work by pointing out that the residents of the building were undoubtedly sympathetic to their cause. It was too late for four of the buildings, but the rest of the block was saved.[37]

In the meantime, City Hall was paralyzed by politics. Police President Acton contacted Mayor George Opdyke,[38] filled him in on the situation, and requested he ask for the Federal garrisons of the harbor forts to send details to help the police. Opdyke did this and also called an emergency meeting of the New York Common Council. But most of the Council were Tammany Hall Democrats, and they knew most of the mob was composed of their voters and supporters. Only half a dozen councilmen showed up, and Opdyke could not get a quorum. Meanwhile, a large, loud, and unfriendly crowd gathered in front of City Hall. The nervous mayor abandoned his office and established a new headquarters at the St. Nicholas Hotel on Broadway and Spring Street.

Anyone who has spent much time in the military knows politics is there, too. General Brown was officially the military commandant of New York City, but the War Department stripped him of all his men except some garrison troops and the Invalid Corps (which was next to useless) and sent them to Gettysburg. Brown was annoyed that Opdyke's request for help was sent to Generals Wool and Sandford but not to him. There was friction between the generals from the beginning.

General Sandford, meanwhile, established himself and his headquarters staff in the arsenal at 7th Avenue and 35th Street. To subdue the mob, he placed advertisements in the afternoon newspapers and had handbills printed, calling up all militiamen who had not yet been sent to Pennsylvania. Obviously, none of this had any immediate effect. He did have one regiment ready to deploy, however. The 10th New York National Guard Regiment was mustered into service that very morning in the Federal Arsenal at Worth and Elm Streets and was preparing to depart for Pennsylvania. Now these orders were cancelled. It was a small unit, having only about five companies instead of the usual ten. Sandford kept two of its companies at the Arsenal (which contained a considerable amount of arms and ammunition). Two other companies were sent to an arsenal

---

37 Headley, pp. 164-65. Details of this incident vary slightly from source to source.

38 George Opdyke was born in New Jersey and lived in Cleveland and New Orleans before settling in New York City. Very prosperous, he owned the largest clothing manufacturing and merchandising company in the area by 1860. A strong Republican and abolitionist, he was elected to the New York State Assembly in 1859 and was a delegate to the 1860 GOP convention, where he supported Abraham Lincoln. Using his own resources, he recruited and equipped Union forces after the war broke out.

near Central Park, and the final company Stanford carried with him to the 7th Avenue Arsenal. The 10th New York was thus deployed in a manner which gave the police no direct help at all. Throughout the riots, General Sandford was more interested in holding the arsenals than in suppressing the rioters.

General Sandford was a man who was very jealous of his prerogatives. He finally appeared at Police Central on Mulberry Street after noon. He was in a stubborn mood and plainly declared that, as the senior military officer in the area after General Wool, he was the commander of all military forces in the city. He demanded that Brown subordinate himself to him and concentrate all of the forces under his command in the 7th Street Arsenal. This Brown refused to do. With Acton's full support, Harvey Brown argued that cooperation with the police was essential, and any concentration should take place at Mulberry Street because the telegraph lines where here, and the police communications center was here. It was clearly the best staging ground for a quick reaction to any situation. The argument became heated, and the arrogant and opinionated Sandford stalked out. He went directly to General Wool, who was also headquartered in the St. Nicholas, and argued with him for some time. Finally the old man yielded and sent a one-sentence dispatch, naming Sandford commander of all forces called out to protect the city. Brown ignored this order and asserted that Sandford could only command militia. He retained command of all Federal troops (mainly men detached from the forts and fortifications), remained at Police Central, and fully cooperated with Acton and the police. In adopting this course of action, he made a valuable contribution to suppressing the riot.

At the War Department, many of his superiors considered Wool "a senile bumbler." He nevertheless reacted better than Sandford. He ordered the commander of Fort Hamilton in New York harbor to send a company and a half (about 150 men) to help the police as soon as possible. He also sent a message to Rear Admiral Hiram Paulding, the commander of the Brooklyn Naval Yard, and asked him to send in detachments of sailors and Marines. Acting on his own initiative, the admiral ordered all his operational naval vessels to take positions in the Hudson and East Rivers and commanded them to be prepared to fire their big guns on the mob if need be. Eventually, Wool even signaled Colonel Alexander Hamilton Bowman, the superintendent of West Point, as well as the governors of New Jersey, Massachusetts, Connecticut and Rhode Island, and the mayor of Newark, for help.[39] He only received reinforcements from Bowman and the governor of New York.

---

39 Headley, pp. 177-78.

* * *

While the generals fussed over prerogatives and the city government did almost nothing, the largest riot in American history continued. Prior to noon, Acton ordered the reserves of 11 different precincts to 3rd Avenue. They could not assemble quickly enough, however, and could do nothing except temporarily hold part of the mob in check. They were not yet ready to fire on the crowd, but they were using their billy clubs (which they called "locust clubs") with more and more gusto.

One grocer, Richard Murphy, saved his store by offering the mob free whiskey. They drank 19 gallons. They also looted a nearby jewelry store. Another group stormed into Thomas Thornton's saloon at 1178 Broadway. They drank all of his liquor, carried off kegs and demijohns of whiskey from the storage room, and robbed him of $200.[40]

At 11:25 a.m., the orders went to the conscription officers: suspend the draft and get all of their equipment and papers to safety. This news affected the mob not at all. It continued its rampage. It had tasted victory, and it wanted more.

---

40 Cook, p. 71.

Police President Thomas C. Acton.

General Harvey Brown

CHAPTER V
JULY 13, 1863: THE FIRST AFTERNOON
THE BATTLE FOR THE ARMORY

By noon on July 13, the streets of New York City were hot, even though the sun was obscured by heavy clouds of smoke as the fires spread. Tempers were short, and the rioters controlled 30 blocks. The mob was exuberant and out of control. They had beaten the police (who initially fought in isolated detachments) in 20 sharp skirmishes. People who were sympathetic to the rioters but were heretofore hesitant now joined them. Plunder and greed made every thief in the city a rioter. Alcohol was also a contributing factor, as was Old World class envy and class hatred. Contempt for a materially superior class of people led to mindless violence. "All well-dressed men and women were in peril if met by the mob," Stoddard recalled.[41] Several men were beaten to death because—and only because—they were well dressed. One witness estimated the size of the mob at 50,000, which was huge. As it moved downtown, it split into three or four sections.

On the other side, off-duty policemen were recalled and were slowly returning to duty. Individual reserve police officers were also coming in. The roughly 400 men of Lieutenant Colonel John Missing's 10th New York National Guard Regiment formed up at the arsenal on White and Elm Streets.[42] This unit included a battery of three 6-pounder cannons. Most of its men were new, ill-

---

41 Stoddard, p. 68.

42 This unit is not to be confused with the 10th New York Infantry Regiment, a/k/a 10th New York Volunteers, which was also later used to suppress the mob.

33

trained, undisciplined recruits, but they could still be used as guards. Missing immediately sent two companies to defend the arsenal at Central Park; shortly thereafter, he sent a third.

At 12:15 p.m., Central Police Headquarters issued a telegram warning there was a danger that a branch of the mob would take the armory at the corner of 21st Street and 2nd Avenue. (This armory was really a rifle manufacturing plant.) There were about operable 500 stands of arms in it.

The building was a large brick structure which was originally a piano factory. Now it manufactured carbines. The entire upper floor was a drill hall for military formations. Nearby, on the corner of 22nd Street and 2nd, was the Union Steam Works building, in which more than 4,000 carbines and rifled muskets were stored. Both buildings contained a small amount of ammunition.

Captain Cameron of the 18th Precinct quickly selected what he dubbed his "Broadway Squad"—32 men under Sergeant Cornelius Burdick. All of these men were six feet tall or taller and physically intimidating. Each was armed with a carbine. Cameron sent them to the armory with orders to hold it at all costs. They infiltrated through the mob singly or in pairs.

Shortly after 1 p.m., a rabble of about 5,000 people attacked the armory. At first, they threw stones through the windows and against the doors, but before long, shots were fired. When the cops did not shoot back initially, the emboldened rioters pushed on the front entrance and shattered the door with a sledge hammer. Instead of allowing them to enter the armory, however, the police opened fire. The lead man was shot in the head and killed. Several others were wounded and carried off by their comrades. The mob was temporarily stunned, but this soon gave way to anger. Sergeant Burdick sent a message to Captain Cameron, asking for help. The captain replied that he had none to send.

By 4 p.m., the mob surged forth again, and it was soon obvious to Sergeant Burdick that he could not hold the armory much longer. Retreat via the front doors was impossible. To escape, the police drove a hole in the rear wall. It was only 1.5 feet in diameter, and they would have to drop 18 feet into the yard below, but to not do so meant death. Every man jumped. They then made their way back to Police Central singly or in groups of two or three. Many of them discarded their uniforms *en route*. The mob did not pursue. They were too busy celebrating and looting the facility.

Inside the building, every member of this segment of the mob armed himself with a carbine. Many of them went upstairs into the drill hall, looking for ammunition and plunder. Meanwhile, those on the lower floors set the armory on fire. Armories contain a great deal of combustible material, including oils

34

and oily rags. The wooden benches and woodwork were made of dry pine and were saturated with oil. The flames reached impressive heights immediately and engulfed the stairs. The rioters on the upper floor (and there were many) were trapped. All of them burned to death. We do not know exactly how many were killed. Later, after the riots were quelled, city workers carried their cadavers from the site. This amounted to little more than skeletal remains, since all the flesh was consumed by the fire. The workers filled barrels with human bones, dumped them in a potters' field or the river, and then refilled the barrels again and again.

Elsewhere, the mob set buildings on fire at the corner of Broadway and 24th Street. They also attacked the Bull's Head Tavern (a/k/a Allerton's Washington Drove Yard Hotel) at 43rd Street and Madison Avenue, near the stockyards, because the proprietor would not give them fire water. They took the liquor and burned down the tavern and hotel, which was four stories high.

THE BATTLE FOR THE MAYOR'S HOME AND THE LAFARGE HOUSE

One of the first objectives of the mob was Mayor Opdyke's residence on 5th Avenue. It was a considerable distance from the original site of the riot, so it is clear that someone targeted it. To his credit, Opdyke made no effort to save his own property, but his friend and neighbor, Captain B. F. Mainerre, the 8th District provost marshal, did. He assembled several well-armed citizens, entered Opdyke's home, and turned it into a fortress.

The first mob to approach was neither large nor determined. Mainerre and Judge George G. Barnard went outside and spoke to them. Their orations and the rifles pointing out the windows caused the rioters to pause. Then Captain John C. Helme of the 27th Precinct appeared with his men and the mob dispersed. A larger and more determined mob appeared later, after Helme and his men were sent to 2nd Avenue, but by then, Captain Wilkins and a detachment of 88 Regulars from Governor's Island showed up, so there was no major attack.

Sometime after 3 p.m., Acton assembled a reserve of 200 men under Inspector Daniel Carpenter. When word arrived that the mob was moving on the home of Mayor Opdyke, he ordered the inspector to go there. (Apparently Acton was not aware that Wilkins' regulars came up.) Carpenter asked Acton what he should do with the prisoners.

"Prisoners?!" the police president snapped. "Don't take any! Kill, kill, kill!" he shouted. "Put down the mob. Don't bring a prisoner in till the mob is put down!"[43]

Meanwhile, the rabble who were checked at the mayor's house marched down Broadway. They intended to sack the Wall Street banks. On route, they wanted to destroy the Lafarge House because it employed a great many African Americans. "Down with property! Down with rich men!" the mob shouted as they marched, and their numbers increased as they advanced. Inspector Carpenter countered by marching his men down Broadway and met the rioters in front of the Lafarge House. The police filled the road from curb to curb and faced the insurgents. Carpenter realized if he gave the mob enough time, it would attack and destroy him. "By the right!" he ordered. "Company front! Double quick! Charge!"

The police waded into the mob, swinging their heavy locust clubs. The mob fought back and numerous sculls were busted. Many wounded men lay on the ground. At least two rioters were killed outright, and others were critically wounded. The rear (follow-up) rank of bluecoats also clubbed the wounded. They took no prisoners. By 5 p.m., the fight was over. Wall Street and the Lafarge House were saved.

THE ORPHANAGE

On the morning of July 13, the mob focused primarily on military targets and government buildings, which were symbols of unfairness to them. By afternoon, however, they turned their wrath against African Americans.

The crowds were huge and the police could not be everywhere at once. While Carpenter and his men fought near the Lafarge House, another segment of the mob (about 3,000 people) attacked the Orphan Asylum for Colored Children on 5th Avenue. It was a large facility, extending from 43rd to 44th Streets. The main structure was four stories high, with two wings of three stories each. It was capable of accommodating 500 children, but only 233 were present on July 13

---

43 Stoddard, p. 80.

The residents of the Colored Orphan Asylum, circa 1861

(New York Historical Society photo)

(excluding staff and employees). All the kids were under the age of 12. As 19th Century orphanages went, this one was luxurious and was well-stocked with food, bedding, and children's clothing.

Orphanage Superintendent William E. Davis saw the mob coming and reacted quickly. He locked the front doors and ordered the staff and children to escape via the rear exits. It worked. The doors held only long enough for the orphans and staff to escape. They sought police protection.

Instead of pursuing, the mob pillaged the orphanage. They took everything: sheets, pillows, blankets, clothing, toys, and food. (In a riot situation, people who have nothing will take anything.)

Chief Engineer John Decker of the Fire Department forced his way into the building and tried to prevent the rioters from burning it. He was knocked down twice and pushed out into the street. By then, the mob was smashing the furniture and lighting fires. Decker and about ten of his men put out the flames on the first and second stories but could not reach the upper floors. More fire engines arrived, but it was too late to save the orphanage and the outbuildings. Everything burned to the ground except Mr. Davis' home, and it was sacked. The firemen did, however, manage to save Chief Engineer Decker.

By late afternoon, the mob turned its attention to the nearby homes, which were inhabited by members of the more prosperous classes. They broke into them and smashed the furniture. Objects of art and luxury were destroyed or tossed into the street. Some of the more practical demonstrators temporarily left the mob and went home, carrying with them the best furniture they would ever own. Others, who secured hatchets and axes by plundering hardware stores, used them to attack pianos, walls, cabinets, and other furnishings. The rioters also burned the home of Abby Hopper Gibbons, a prison reformer and daughter of a famous abolitionist. They attacked Ann Martin (a white woman who married a black man), as well as a white prostitute who catered to African American men. Near the rivers, white longshoremen destroyed dance halls, brothels, boarding houses, and other businesses which Negroes patronized.[44]

Meanwhile, the orphans were taken to the 22nd Precinct station house, which was at least reasonably safe. The older orphans carried the younger ones on their backs. They spent the night in the station house.

44 Charles River, n.p.

The Colored Orphan Asylum before the riots.

The Colored Orphan Asylum on fire, 1863.

OTHER ATTACKS

Negroes were being attacked all over the city. Lieutenant Colonel Arthur Fremantle of the Coldstream Guards was in New York, awaiting passage back to the United Kingdom, when he was astonished to see a crowd chasing an African American, screaming "Down with the bloody niggers!" and "Kill all niggers!" The shocked British colonel asked a bystander "what the negroes had done that they should want to kill them?"

"Oh, sir, they hate them here," came the reply. "They are the innocent cause of all these troubles."[45]

Around 4:30 p.m., another part of the multitude attacked the Enrollment Office at Broadway and 29th. It was defended by a mixed military/police force of inadequate size. The mob defeated the soldiers/police and stormed into the building. The draft officials already abandoned the place and took their papers with them. The horde carried the furniture into the street and set it on fire, along with the office building and a few nearby structures. They also looted several stores, including a jewelry store. The mob, Stoddard recalled, acted "with a barbarian zest worthy of the Huns of Attila."[46] By 5 p.m., 11 buildings on the 1100 block of Broadway were on fire. A block of new houses on 3rd Avenue and 44th Street were also plundered and burned.

The riots in the lower wards did not begin until late afternoon. Most of the attacks here were racially motivated. One mob assaulted a building on Baxter Street because it was occupied by African Americans, but police from the 6th Precinct dispersed them. An hour later they checked an attack on Crook's Restaurant on Nassau Street, which was in danger because it employed black waiters, but again the mob was stopped by the 6th. At 6 p.m., a building at the corner of Leonard and Baxter was struck because it housed about 20 black families. Several better residences were pillaged and jewelry stores were robbed.

---

45 Arthur Fremantle, *Three Months in the Southern States* (New York: 1864), p. 300. Fremantle had just returned from observing Robert E. Lee's army at Gettysburg.

46 Stoddard, p. 89.

As night fell, all the saloons in the effected area were crowded and doing a land office business. Most of the patrons got their fill of bad whiskey and then rejoined the mob. At 6 p.m., the 8th Precinct signaled Police Central and reported: "They are driving all the n***gers out of the ward, as soon as they show on the streets." The precinct called for reinforcements.[47]

At 6:15 p.m., the 8th attacked the mob with billy clubs and temporarily dispersed the crowd. But it merely reassembled somewhere else.

In the 18th Precinct, meanwhile, Captain Cameron reported the situation was "very bad." Most of the streets in the ward were under the control of the horde. Shortly after, he ordered the station house abandoned. The mob promptly ransacked it.

The situation in the 4th Precinct also continued to deteriorate. The mob stoned the station house, and the police responded with musket fire. At 7:45 p.m., Precinct Captain James Bryan signaled that the rioters were attacking and burning African American boarding houses, and he did not have enough men to prevent it. Moments later, the wire went dead. Bryan sent a man to the 26th Precinct, who borrowed their telegraph and signaled that the 4th needed help badly.

Communications with the 4th Precinct were restored at 9 p.m. Bryan reported that the situation was disastrous. Two severely injured African Americans were brought into the station house, but they were almost dead.

Another mob attacked the New York *Tribune* building across from City Hall at 7:55 p.m. Defenses were weak, and the mob overran the first floor. About ten minutes later, police from Captain Thomas W. Torne's 26th (City Hall) Precinct and most of the men of Captain Jacob B. Warlow's 1st Precinct arrived and drove out the vandals, but they reported the *Tribune* office was "gutted."[48] Inspector Carpenter and his 200 men were also ordered to this area. They spent the night in City Hall. Meanwhile, at 10:25 p.m., the 6th Precinct reported a large mob was destroying the dwellings of black people on Park Street. Ten minutes later, the 13th Precinct telegraphed that a mob had set Duffy's Place (Number 429 Grand Street, at the corner of Grand and Ridge Streets) on fire. This was where

---

47 *Ibid*, p. 99.

48 Stoddard, p. 106; Headley, pp. 179-80. The total strength of the police force was estimated at 150.

the Enrollment Office was located. Elsewhere in the darkness, Colonel Nugent's house and that of Postmaster Abram Wakeman were burned. Wakeman was a well-known Republican and big Lincoln supporter.[49]

At 10:50 p.m., 1st Precinct signaled taking in a great many Negroes, in order to protect them from the demonstrators. This was not anything special; every other station house was doing the same. On the west side (lower downtown) on Clarkson Street near the Hudson, an unoffending black man was beaten and kicked by the mob. After torturing him for some time, they hanged him from a tree and set a fire under his feet while he struggled for life. At 11:45 p.m., Police President Acton telegraphed the 28th Precinct and asked if he was still hanging. He was. Acton ordered Precinct Captain John F. Dickson to cut him down. Forty minutes later, Dickson signaled that the mob would not allow his men anywhere near the body. The mob also killed Peter Heuston, a 63--year-old Mohawk Indian. Because of his dark complexion, he was mistaken for a Negro.

A half hour before midnight, a heavy rain began to fall. It cooled off the oppressive heat, put out some of the fires, ran the rioters indoors, and ended the first day of the riot. But everyone knew there would be a second day.

---

49 Abram Wakeman (b. 1824) was an attorney and a wealthy businessman, with interests in railroads, banks, and insurance companies. He was a crony of Secretary of State William Seward and Thurlow Weed. Initially a Whig (like Lincoln), he helped form the GOP in 1854. Wakeman served in the New York State Assembly (1850-52), on the Board of Aldermen (1854-55), and as a U.S. Congressman (1855-57). He was defeated for reelection in 1856. In 1861, he raised the 81st Pennsylvania Infantry Regiment and briefly served as its colonel but resigned before it left for the war. Entitled to patronage, Lincoln named him city postmaster in 1862.

NEW YORK—THE COLORED ORPHAN ASYLUM, 143D STREET. THE FORMER
BUILDING DESTROYED DURING THE DRAFT RIOTS OF 1863.

CHAPTER VI
THE SECOND DAY

Riot fever was spreading on the morning of Tuesday, July 14. Police and military reinforcements had not yet arrived in sufficient numbers to have much impact on the situation, and the lukewarm thought the mob was winning. Some of these were enticed to join the riot by the prospect of easy plunder.

Although it was not obvious, the military took charge of the edges of the riot zone. All of the approaches to the Naval Yard were covered by the gunboat *North Carolina* (40 guns); the corvette *Savannah* (22 guns); the gunboats *Granite City*, *Gertrude*, and *Unadilla* (8 guns each); and the *Tulip* (6 guns). The steamer tug *Fuchsia* (one 30-pounder rifle and one 24-pounder howitzer) and the *Passaic*, a single turreted coastal monitor, were posted off the southern extremity of Manhattan. The armories were also now secure. The 7th Regiment Armory was held by 400 men and two howitzers. One hundred men from the Invalid Corps, plus sailors and marines, took positions on Worth Street, near Broadway. Colonel Bliss, with a strong force and a battery of guns, defended the Sub-Treasury Building. But elsewhere the rioters ran amuck. Early that morning, the mob burned the Washington Hall Hotel and building in Harlem, before proceeding to a mill on 129th Street. The bridge over the Harlem River at McComb's Dam was also destroyed by arsonists.

Meanwhile, the mob barricaded the area between 11th and 14th Streets, which became something of a fortified mobilization headquarters for the gangs. Telegraph poles were cut down and placed across the streets. Carts, boxes, city street sweepers and lumber were used to form barricades.

The establishment forces also built up their strength. At 7:45 a.m., Police Central received a message from General Stanford informing them that Colonel Henry O'Brien of the 11th New York previously sent 150 men and two 6-pounders with 25 artillerists to the scene of the riot. They were a mixed bag of volunteers and militia. Meanwhile, the morning editions of the newspapers hit the streets. All of them contained a plea from Mayor Opdyke, asking for all loyal citizens to report to Police Headquarters at 300 Mulberry Street, where they would be sworn in as special policemen. Generals Wool and Stanford called upon veterans to volunteer for special military service.

The turnout was good. Many of the veterans recently completed two years' enlistments (most of it on the Eastern Front) but were willing to return to the colors in an emergency. Numerous volunteers formed up at the 7th Regiment Armory and were placed under the command of Colonel J. M. Davis. Others were organized by Colonel Allen of the 1st New York Infantry Regiment; Lieutenant Colonel Ashley of the 37th New York National Guard; Colonel Taylor of the 4th New York; Major Wales of the 17th Chasseurs; Colonel Howard of the 12th Heavy Artillery; Lieutenant Colonel Robert F Allason of the 38th New York National Guard; and Colonel Edward Jardine, 9th New York Infantry Regiment, aka "Hawkins Zouaves;" and Colonel Frank Jones, 31st New York.

Several of these veteran units were exceedingly swift to reconstitute themselves, albeit it in reduced numbers. The 38th New York was one. It spent two years with the Army of the Potomac but was mustered out on June 22, 1863, at East New York. It lost 59 men killed during the 1861-1863 period. Elements of the 9th New York were also especially quick to respond. The regiment was already in the process of re-mustering and was in an advanced state of preparation on July 13. An ad hoc regiment of veterans was formed under Colonel Cleveland Winslow of the Duryea Zouaves, while a battle group of the 13th Volunteer Heavy Artillery fell in at the Elm Street Armory. It included three field pieces. After being caught flat-footed by the outbreak of the riot, the U.S. military forces were regaining their balance with incredible speed.

In the meantime, early on July 14, in the theater of the absurd, City Judge John H. McCunn declared the Draft Law unconstitutional. The idea that a corrupt city judge could legislate from the bench and declare unconstitutional a Federal law passed by the U.S. Congress is ridiculousness *per se*, but at least Judge McCunn was trying to solve the problem, even if he was acting far above his pay grade. His ruling had no impact upon events, however.

On July 14, the mob was probably stronger than the day before. "The consternation in the streets seemed to be on the increase," Colonel Fremantle recalled. "Fires were going on in all directions and the streets were being patrolled by large bodies of police followed by special constables, the latter bearing truncheons, but not looking very happy."[50]

---

50 Fremantle, pp. 301-02.

Martha Perry remembered: "Men, both colored and white, were murdered within two blocks of us, some being hung to the nearest lamppost, and others shot. An army officer was walking in the street near our house, when a rioter was seen to kneel on the sidewalk, take aim, fire and kill him, then coolly start on his way, unmolested." The whole day, she said, was "fearful."[51]

In the meantime, the gang warlords and ringleaders were raking in the cash. Businesses, factories, hotels, and even railroads were paying them handsomely not to burn their property.[52] Obviously, exact figures are impossible to obtain, but the amounts must have been considerable.

At 8:30 a.m., a mob congregated at 2nd Avenue and 34th Street. Another came together in the vicinity of South Street. At 9:10 a.m., about 2,000 rioters left the corner of 31st Street and 10th Avenue and headed downtown. Five minutes later, 21st Precinct reported that a mob had burned one or two buildings on 2nd Avenue and 34th Street. Once again, circumstances required the police to react quickly. By now, however, they were better prepared. Stagecoaches and carriages were impressed into public service, as were street and railroad cars, and they moved the police rapidly. This method also had the advantage of sparing the cops long marches in hot weather, so they weren't as fatigued when they arrived. This time, the coaches transferred Inspector Daniel Carpenter and about 300 men.

A few minutes before 10 a.m., there was sharp fighting on 2nd Avenue between 34th and 35th Streets. Rioters hurled rocks from rooftops into police ranks, while other insurrectionists closed in on their rear. Swinging their billy clubs, the officers fought their way out of the trap. Carpenter sent several policemen to the top of the roof of a four-story building, Led by Captain John I. Mount of the 11th Precinct, they tossed a few of the rock-throwers to the pavement below. It is doubtful if any of these men survived. Of the police, General Brown commented: "I never saw such drill and discipline in all my life, and I was born in the Army."[53]

About 10 a.m., the police were joined by Colonel O'Brien and two companies of the 11th New York Infantry Regiment, including a section of artillery under Lieutenant Eagleson. They fired into the crowd at close range. Seven rioters were

---

51 Charles River, n.p.

52 Headley, p. 224.

53 Stoddard, p. 145.

killed outright in the first volley, including a woman with a child in her arms, and many others were wounded. This broke up the 2nd Avenue concentration. At the same time, on Delancey Street, a company of regulars (about 150 men) under Lieutenant Wood was surrounded and attacked by a mob of about 3,000 people. The soldiers fired several volleys at almost point-blank range. The mob fell back. Wood proceeded to Pitt Street, where he was surrounded again. Once more, he fired volleys in the crowd at close range, again killing or wounding numerous rioters. The exact numbers, however, are not known.

Colonel O'Brien reported to Lieutenant Colonel Frothingham (Brown's second-in-command) with about 30 men and offered his services. Forthingham, however, realized that O'Brien was "under the influence" and declined his help. The colonel saved face by asking to be excused on the grounds of sickness. Forthingham granted his request. O'Brien then disbanded his detachment but personally returned to the scene of the riot.

Writing in 1873, author Joel Tyler Headley gives us a sample of the chaotic situation facing Acton, Brown, and their men by recording the most important telegrams received by and dispatched from Police Central. They included:

(10:20 a.m.): from 13th Precinct: send military reinforcements immediately.

(10:22 a.m.): to the 7th Precinct: find soldiers and send them to 13th Street forthwith.

(10:45 a.m.): from 16th Precinct: a mob has just attacked Jones Soap Factory.

(10:45 a.m.): to 26th Precinct (City Hall): send 100 officers to Police Central immediately.

(10:55 a.m.): to 20th Precinct from General Brown: a heavy battle is going on at the arsenal. Captain Wilkins and a company of regulars is to report to me at Police Central at once.

(11:18 a.m.): from 16th Precinct: mob is approaching station house. "We have no men."

(11:20 a.m.): from 18th Precinct: A "very wild" mob is at the corner of 22nd Street and 2nd Avenue. They have attacked the Union Steam Factory (see below).

(11:35 a.m.): from 20th Precinct: send another 100 men immediately.

(11:38 a.m.): to 21st Precinct: can you send a few men to Police Central?

(11:40 a.m.): from 22nd Precinct: the mob is heading to Mr. Higgins' factory at the foot of 43rd Street to burn it (see below).

(11:45 a.m.): from 18th Precinct: mob here is about 4,500 strong. What shall we do? ANSWER: "Clear [Calm ?] them down, if you can."

(11:50 a.m.): from 18th Precinct: we must leave. The mob is here with guns.

(11:50 a.m.): from 20th Precinct: mob tearing up railroad tracks on 11th Avenue.

(11:58 a.m.): from 13th Precinct: mob has sacked a large gun store on Grant Street and are on their way to attack us (see below).

(12:10 p.m.): to 15th Precinct: send your men here forthwith.

(12:35 p.m.): from 20th Precinct: send 200 men to 35th Street arsenal immediately.

(12:36 p.m.): from 21st Precinct: mob just broke into a gun store on 3rd Avenue between 36th and 37th Streets.

(12:40 p.m.): from 21st Precinct: send help. Situation "desperate."[54]

At 10:35 a.m., the mob threatened Delamater Iron Works on 14th Street. Why the mob menaced this plant is unknown: it manufactured steam-boilers. In any case, the military, including a company of Marines, arrived. At 10:40 a.m. the Marines fired into the crowd, inflicting quite a few casualties.

So it went all morning. At 10:50 a.m., the 16th Precinct telegraphed that all the stores on 8th Avenue were closing due to fear of the mob on 17th Street. Acton responded by asking General Sandford to send troops to 8th Avenue and 17th Street.

About that time, someone suggested to Police President Acton that his men use muskets. He rejected the idea out of hand, pointing out that the policemen were excellent and thoroughly drilled in the use of the club, but not with a rifle. Using muskets would only turn good policemen into poor militia. They were, however, well trained in the use of the revolver, and sometimes employed it very effectively.

Back in Washington, D.C., Secretary of War Edwin Stanton had a panic attack. He was afraid New York City was about to join the Confederacy. He was in constant communication with Edward S. Sanford, the head of the U.S. Military Telegraph Service in the city, asking all kinds of questions Sanford could not answer.

Abraham Lincoln, on the other hand, kept his head. He refused to declare martial law, correctly reasoning that Federal overreach caused the problem (i.e., the riot); overt Federal intrusion at this point would only exacerbate the crisis. Better, he decided, to let the state and city handle it. Of course, he could and did assist them by sending Federal troops to the area.

Meanwhile, at 10:40 a.m., the 21st Precinct reported the military was firing minie balls into the crowd, but the cannons were firing blanks only. This tactic cleared the streets, but the mob gathered almost as quickly at other points. Several of the rioters were killed or badly wounded. The precinct captain felt the authorities were getting the better of the fighting.

---

54 Headley, pp. 203-05.

Before long, there were several skirmishes going on at once. The situation deteriorated to the point that the army gunners started firing grape and canister into the mob. Still the angry civilians pressed forward. Police reported men in expensive suits of clothes were being beaten by the crowd. Some of them were killed.

One prong of the mob boarded a British vessel in the harbor, pushed aside the captain, and "cruelly beat his colored crew," Colonel Fremantle recorded. There was no British man-of-war present, so the captain appealed to a French admiral, who allowed all British ships with Negro crews to anchor under the protection of his frigate.[55]

Back at City Hall, Governor Horatio Seymour arrived and issued a proclamation, declaring New York City in a state of insurrection. He called on Archbishop John Hughes, an Irishmen, to exert his influence and call upon the Catholic rioters to cease and desist. Hughes did so, but his appeal was lukewarm and did not appear in the newspapers until Wednesday morning.

Meanwhile, the New York Stock Exchange, the Merchants' Exchange, the U.S. Sub-Treasury, and the Union League Club all organized troops of volunteers. Among them was William O. Stoddard, one of Lincoln's private secretaries, who was in the city on vacation. Each formed volunteer companies of about 100 men. At the same time, steamboats brought reinforcements and cannons from Riker's Island and Governor's Island, while a Zouaves company from the 84th New York Militia took charge of the city armory at the corner of White and Elm Streets, and the 10th National Zouaves and some howitzers arrived to defend the Sub-Treasury and Custom House, along with 150 armed citizen volunteers.

At 11:30 a.m., the 20th Precinct reported the mob was tearing up the New York Central and Hudson River Railroad tracks on 11th Avenue. Obviously not considering this a priority crisis, Acton merely instructed that General Sandford be informed.

Five minutes later, 20th Precinct telegraphed that Union Steam Factory was under attack. Acton ordered Captain George W. Walling to send 100 men to the facility. This order was impossible to obey. The mob took the factory. Acton also ordered the 20th to send 100 men to disperse a crowd at Mayor Opdyke's house. It was again being threatened, and the mob was throwing rocks through the window. The precinct sent what it could.

---

55 Fremantle, p. 302.

Twenty minutes before noon, the 18th Precinct telegraph operator signaled that he had to leave. The mob was there with guns. Acton sent a company to their station house on 22nd Street near 2nd Avenue.

Five minutes later, the 22nd Precinct reported the mob went to Higgins' Carpet Factory at 43rd Street to burn it. At 11:58 a.m., Captain Thomas Steers of the 13th Precinct signaled that the mob just sacked a large gun store on Grand Street and was heading for the station house to attack it. The battle was sharp and short. At 12:05 p.m., the 13th Precinct police and a supporting detachment of marines gave way. This marked the first time a military force was defeated by the mob.

Meanwhile, at noon, the *Tribune* reported from the corner of Broadway and 23rd Street. The heart of New York was dead. There were no people, except a few lying on the pavement. The air was so full of smoke one could scarcely breathe. Scores of men were beaten half to death for wearing good clothes. Business ceased altogether. Unloading and loading of cargo ships stopped. All the streetcar lines ceased to operate. Most of the telegraph lines were down. According to the *Tribune*, the rioters set 24 major fires since the previous morning. Whole blocks of buildings were burned. The mob was carrying guns, pistols, axes, hatchets, crowbars, pitchforks, knives, bludgeons, and the Red Flag. "Down with the rich men!" they cried. "Down with property! Down with the police."[56]

At the same time, part of the West Side mob pushed down 6th Avenue with the intention of burning No. 37, the residence of a prominent GOP politician. They were met by police from the 20th Precinct and a company of Regulars under Captain Putnam. They were repulsed and pushed back to 5th Avenue. Here, Putnam ordered a bayonet charge. The police (on Putnam's flanks) used their locustwood clubs. The mob scattered.

---

56 Stoddard, p. 10.

CHAPTER VII
THE SECOND AFTERNOON

Troubles without ceasing poured onto the head of Police President Acton, who had not slept since Sunday. Captain Walling of the 20th Precinct signaled at 12:40 p.m. that Allerton's Hotel on 11th Avenue was sacked and burning. This mob was also tearing up railroad tracks because they knew soldiers would be coming soon and might be on their way already. They also knew they would be coming by rail.

At 12:45 p.m., General Sandford telegraphed Central Office and asked Colonel Nugent, the provost-marshal, to send him 200 good troopers immediately because the 7th Regiment Arsenal was threatened. Sandford had 1,000 men there on Monday evening, but almost all of them were sent out. Nugent had only a detachment of the Invalid Corps under his command. He could send no succor.

The 21st Precinct called for help again at 12:50. All its men were in the streets, and the station house was vulnerable. Acton replied he would send aid as soon as he could.

There were now 1,200 Special Police on duty. The "Specials" had almost no training or experience in police work. They were nevertheless used effectively, mostly in defending station-houses, and in doing so, they freed up regular police for more arduous duties. Supplying the police, the Specials, and troops with provisions was also an issue. The men were tired and, in many cases, hungry. But the riot roared on. At 1:08 p.m., 20th Precinct reported the mob was looting gunsmiths in the precinct. Captain Walling suggested they take possession of all arms in places not yet under attack. Acton rejected this idea because he could neither secure them nor transport them out of the danger zone.

At 1:18 p.m., Captain James Bryan's 4th Precinct called for help and stated the mob was about to break into the gun store on Catherine Street. The rabble proved very effective at arming itself. Fortunately, there were so many different types of rifles, pistols, muskets, and other firearms that finding sufficient quantities of the ammunition that matched a certain gun proved impossible. This simple logistical fact may have been all that saved New York City. The mob had no General Staff officers.

There was plenty of trouble in any case. Arthur Fremantle recalled: "The reports of outrages, hangings, and murder, were now most alarming, the terror and anxiety were universal. All shops were shut: all carriages and omnibuses had ceased running. No man or woman of color was visible or safe in the streets, or even their own dwellings. Telegraphs were cut, and railroad tracks torn up . . . the mob evidently had the upper hand."[57]

At 1:30 p.m., 20th Precinct reported the large feed store on 9th Avenue near 29th Street was on fire, thanks to the mob. Shortly after 2 p.m., the 20th reported the gangs were taking horses from the Red Bird Line stables. Apparently, the mob actually tried to form a cavalry outfit but were not successful.

At 2:30 p.m., 7th Precinct signaled that a large crowd (500 men) assembled at the corner of Market and Monroe Streets and were demolishing an African American shanty. No reinforcements were available. The mob had its way. At the same time, Captain Johannes C. Slott's 22nd Precinct reported the military arrived and fired on the mob at the corner of 10th Avenue and 44th Street.

It should be mentioned the German areas caused the police virtually no trouble during the entire week. They were typical Germans: clean, well-ordered, hard-working, and submissive to authority. They were also well-organized. (Of course they were: they were Germans.) Their leaders informed the police on July 13, they would cause no trouble, and they did not. They organized their own unofficial neighborhood watches (which totaled about 1,000 men), and freed police for employment elsewhere. It is a good thing they were docile. They were the second largest immigrant group in the city, and they numbered more than 110,000 people. Had the Germans rioted, the police and military forces would not have been able to handle them. As of yet, the situation was far from under control; the authorities were unable to handle the Irish.

Fighting continued on 2nd Avenue above 20th Street, near the ruins of the 21st Street Armory, which was still smoking. The Union Steam Works (also called the "wire factory"), which contained 4,000 carbines, was here and still occupied by the mob.

---

57 Fremantle, p. 302.

About 10 a.m., Inspector George W. Dilks was ordered to take command of approximately 200 police (including most of the patrolmen from Captain Jeremiah Petty's 5th Precinct) and to clear 2nd Avenue and recapture the wire factory. He launched a close-order charge and pushed forward against fierce resistance. Hand-to-hand fighting and terrible clubbings took place. Many policemen were also hurt and several were seriously wounded but none fatally. The mob fled, leaving most of the carbines and their plunder behind. Among the dead was the mob's leader. Captain Henry Hedden, the commander of the 16th Precinct, examined the body. To everyone's surprise, Hedden discovered he was "a young man of delicate features and fair, white skin." He was dressed as a laborer but this was obviously a disguise, because underneath his dirty shirt and overalls he wore fine cassimere pants, a fine vest, and an expensive linen shirt. His identity was never learned. His body disappeared in a subsequent skirmish and was secretly buried somewhere, like so many others.[58]

It was 2 p.m. before the police reached the entrance, and then they had to capture the interior. More severe close-quarter fighting occurred. One physician later reported that he treated 21 head wounds made by police locust clubs. All were fatal. There were also many lessor wounds, and this doctor wasn't the only one treating such injuries.

In the meantime, the police piled the recaptured weapons high on a large express-wagon. Each policeman carried what he could, but they couldn't carry them all. They headed for Police Central. Along the way, people cheered them.

Seeking to take advantage of the momentum, Dilks decided to clear the neighborhood. Rioters hurled rocks and bricks down on them from the upper stories. One rioter was shot and killed just as he threw a brick.

Dilks's column passed through 22nd Street into 1st Avenue, where it collided with another part of the mob, which hurled paving stones on the Regulars. Captain Franklin ordered them to disperse, but they refused. He then fired several volleys into the crowd, and there were many casualties.

The mixed police/army column advanced another block before it met a strong force of rioters at 2nd Avenue and 21st Street. They again fired repeated volleys and eventually were able to proceed toward Police Central and safety. Meanwhile, the rioters reoccupied the five-story wire factory and burned it to the ground.

---

58 Headley, p. 201.

Dilks and his men reached Police Central at 3 p.m. After he reported, Captain Helm and some General Headquarters men, along with a detachment from the 18th Precinct, were sent back to the wire factory to retrieve the rest of the carbines. They were soon surrounded by the mob and in trouble. Dilks set out with his 200 men to rescue them. He was supported by a company of Regular infantry under Captain Franklin. They arrived just in time to save Helms and his men, who were about to be overwhelmed. They retook the wire factory and seized the remaining weapons.

Fire alarm bells were ringing constantly as terror gripped the streets. This was especially true for the African American population, which was a prime target of the mob since the riots began. Those who could crowded the ferry landings seeking escape. Headley recalled: "A sight of one [Negro] in the streets would call forth a halloo, as when a fox breaks cover, and away would dash a half a dozen men in pursuit . . . If overtaken, he was pounded to death at once; if he escaped into a negro house for safety, it was set on fire, and the inmates made to share a common fate. Deeds were done and sights were witnessed that one would not have dreamed of, except among savage tribes."[59]

One black man was stripped naked and killed at the corner of 27th Street and 7th Avenue. Several Irishmen danced around the body, "shouting like wild Indians."[60] Stores which catered to African Americans were looted, two black boarding houses were smashed and then burned, and a Negro barber shop was torched. "Old men, seventy years of age, and young children, too young to comprehend what it all meant, were cruelly beaten and killed," one observer recorded. "The spirit of hell seemed to have entered the hearts of these men . . ."[61]

At 2:20 p.m., the 20th Precinct reported that the army had arrived, defeated and dispersed the mob. One soldier was wounded and captured—and probably soon killed. But the situation here was still desperate and the telegram was premature. At 2:50, the police were fighting for the 20th Precinct Station House. Captain Walling requested reinforcements. The fighting was still in progress at 4:25.

Acton signaled 6th Precinct at 3:25 p.m. that it should look out for Baxter Street, the mob was going to burn some Negro dwellings. Apparently it did so.

---

59 Headley, pp. 206-07.

60 *Ibid.*, p. 207.

61 *Ibid.*, p. 208.

At 4:25 p.m., 16th Precinct Captain Hedden signaled Police Central that he had just left the 20th Precinct. The mob was about to attack the station house. General Brown apparently ordered the soldiers in the area to return to West 35th Street, where they turned back the mob.

That same afternoon, part of the mob marched to the hospital on 41st Street (near Lexington Avenue) to burn it down possibly because there were 250 wounded Union soldiers here. The hospital was rescued by armed citizens after a sharp skirmish.

Another part of the mob entered the grounds of Columbia College to destroy it. (Only the rich and well-to-do attended college in those days.) They were confronted by a Roman Catholic priest, who spoke boldly and eloquently. The mob, which was made up of Irish Roman Catholics, would actually listen to a priest. They turned around and left. Unfortunately, the priest's name was never recorded for posterity.

Late that afternoon, the mob in the vicinity of Pitt and Delancey Streets again attacked African American dwellings. A detachment of U.S. Marines was sent to stop them. The mob surrounded the marines, who responded by opening fire. A dozen rioters were killed outright, and many more were wounded.

The mob's proclivity for violence seemed to have no limits. A public school house in the 16th Precinct was attacked because a couple of black women the mob was pursuing fled there. The teachers and students barricaded the doors and held their positions until help came. Someone said a house opposite the school belonged to African American people. That was enough. The mob demolished it. Many Negroes were beaten senseless and lay unconscious on the street for hours. Two black children at 59 Thompson Street were simply shot out of hand. Both died instantly.[62]

Elsewhere, Aaron Haxter's hardware store (Number 78 Avenue B) was looted, as was John Wagner's lock and gunsmith store at 65 Avenue A. Thomas Egan's tailor shop on Avenue A was also completely stripped of his merchandise. About the same time, on the waterfront, rioters hanged William Jones and burned his body. Dock workers beat another African-American and almost drowned him. They beat Jeremiah Robinson to death and threw his body into the river. William Williams, a black sailor, was stabbed and stoned to death,

---

62 Charles River, n.p.

his body horribly mutilated. Abraham Franklin, a Negro coachman, was taken from his apartment and hanged from a lamppost. As he "danced on air," the crowd cheered for President Davis.[63]

African American James Costello ran away, but the mob chased him. Costello turned and shot the leader, but the rest of the mob overwhelmed him. Six white men then beat, stomped, and kicked him to death.

Meanwhile, Colonel O'Brien of the 11th New York, who was hit in the knee by a stone, returned to his home, which was located on 2nd Avenue, between 34th and 35th Streets. This was a rash act on his part. (This might be explained because he had been drinking.) His family had already moved to safer parts, the house was sacked by rioters, and he wanted to assess the damage. But he should have taken a strong detachment of men with him.

O'Brien traveled alone. Accounts vary slightly, but thugs (which included some women) were waiting for him. They captured him, tortured him savagely, dragged him outside by the hair on his head, and beat him mortally.

A drugstore owner saw this vicious act and brought the dying colonel a glass of water. The mob then sacked and burned his store.

Other witnesses and neighbors carried the dying colonel to a nearby house, but the mob returned at nightfall and dragged him out again. A brave priest interrupted the proceedings and administrated the last rites. (The mob had not reached the point where they would attack men of the cloth.) This priest and another man lifted him into a handbarrow and carried him to Bellevue Hospital, but it was too late. Colonel O'Brien was already dead.

Because his neighbors tried to help O'Brien, the mob burned down the entire row of nearby houses. The warning was clear: those who opposed mob rule would be punished.

Meanwhile, at 5:40 p.m., 21st Precinct reported the horde was breaking into and burning stores on 2nd and 3rd Avenue, near 40th Street. They also attacked the 20th Precinct station house, which was now quite crowded with policemen and people from the Colored Orphanage. The police met them with clubs, and soldiers shot to kill. The mob fled.

The forces of the establishment won some victories that day, but the mob still controlled much of the city. The telegraph service was a mess: many lines were down and there was chaos. The military and the police held what amounted to tactical islands. The mob operated freely in the intervening spaces.

---

63 *Ibid.*, n.p.

Colonel Henry O'Brien (1825-1863). A native of Ireland, he was beaten to death by the mob Initially buried in a pauper's grave, he was later moved to Calvary Cemetery, Queens, and buried next to his children, who predeceased him.

(https://www.findagrave.com/memorial/176165469/henry-f_-o_brien).

On the other hand, communications between the civilian police and regular military units was excellent. General Brown commanded the regular forces, and he kept Acton completely informed of military movements. Both Acton and Brown sent out spies, and they kept them abreast of the mob's movements and—to some extent—of their immediate objectives. At least 16 detectives worked the mob as spies. Only one was identified by the rioters. He was beaten but, fortunately for him, not too badly.

At 6:10 p.m., the 21st Precinct (located on West 35th Street) advised Police Central they expected another attack after dark and asked for help, if Acton could provide any. He promised to send men from the 16th Precinct once the situation was stabilized there. Ten minutes later, the 28th Precinct signaled that a company of soldiers attacked the mob at 29th Street but were repulsed.

Several minor reversals followed, mainly because the mob was better armed than at the beginning. They even had a few cannons and tried to form what amounted to an artillery contingent. They were not very successful because they lacked ammunition for their guns and had no experienced gunners or spotters, although they did reportedly get off a few rounds.

At 6:35 p.m., the 20th Precinct telegraphed Police Central: the throng was planning to burn the bombshell factory at 24th Street and 10th Avenue as well as other factories. The mob had blocked the streets with carts. Police President Acton was busy, however, trying to save the block of buildings at 2nd Avenue and 34th Street, but he had no men to send and could not raise any. His forces were simply stretched too thin and could not be everywhere at once.

Both soldiers and police were nearing exhaustion. Many of them had done extremely stressful work for two days and were badly in need of rest, but they had no choice except to keep going. Some calls for relief could not be honored. At 7:10 p.m., for example, Captain Henry Hedden of the 16th Precinct objected to dispatching its remaining soldiers and policemen against the mob. If it did, he said, the mob would burn the station house. At 10:30 p.m., the 10th Precinct reported several fires, but it lacked the men to deal with them. (This precinct was quiet most of the day.)

By this time, almost every station house was without soldiers, who were in the streets and often operating independently. The buildings were improvised fortresses defended by police, Specials, and citizens.

New York City was fortunate there was no wind that night to spread the fires. The fire department generally performed well on July 14, despite the fact that many of its members sympathized with the mob.

At 8:40 p.m., Acton ordered 26th Precinct (which was headquartered at City Hall) to send a force to the corner of Catherine and Cherry Streets because Brooks Brothers clothing store was under attack. Precinct Captain Thomas W. Thorne signaled back that he did not have enough men to comply, so Acton sent them reinforcements from the 4th Precinct. These lawmen rushed a force to the Brooks store and initially repulsed the mob, but it returned. By 10:05 p.m., the police were defeated. The mob did not pursue. They were too busy trying on fashionable suits and other clothing none of them could afford in normal times. The store was completely looted. Acton sent even more reinforcements, so the cops regrouped and retook the store (or what was left of it) at 11:22 p.m.

The 5th Precinct learned, meanwhile, that its station house was in danger because it was sheltering about 400 African Americans. Assisted by black Specials, the police barricaded the doors. But the mob attacked elsewhere. At 10:35 p.m., the 5th reported the crowd was demolishing an entire row of buildings on York Street.

An attack began on the 26th Precinct at 10 p.m. The mob was attempting to set the building on fire when Inspector Carpenter arrived with his roving battle group, which took the mob in the rear, and dispersed it. Seven minutes later, 26th Precinct signaled that Carpenter's men met the mob on Broadway, whipped them, and the survivors scattered in all directions.

Throughout the evening, and indeed for the rest of the week, the gas-houses and gas-works received top priority. Most of them were garrisoned. The gas-works on the North River at 42nd Street, however, were not thought to be in danger, so it was given only a token defensive force. The mob (which preferred to operate in darkness) attacked it and destroyed it, putting out the lights in part of the city. Meanwhile, the throng sacked the house of James Sinclair of the Tribune (on 29th Street). They were looking for Horace Greeley.[64]

At 10:45 p.m., the 29th Precinct reported they needed immediate assistance. The mob was breaking into private homes, robbing them, and setting them on fire. Acton sent them reinforcements right away.

The 18th Precinct reported its station house (on 22nd Street near 2nd Avenue) was on fire at 11:20 p.m. Shortly after, the mob captured the building. They looted it as thoroughly as they could before the flames forced them to abandon it. It burned to the ground.

---

64 Sinclair and Greeley were related.

Meanwhile, the mob broke into the cellar apartment of the Derrickson family on Worth Street. As they broke down the door, Mr. Derrickson (who was black) fled out the back window, apparently thinking the mob would not attack his wife (who was white) or their two children. He was wrong. They beat Ann and her son Alfred with an ax and the spoke of a wagon wheel. Mrs. Derrickson threw her body over that of her son and screamed, "For God sake, kill me and save my boy!" The rabble would not listen, however. They left the critically wounded mother on the floor and pulled Albert out into the street, where they beat him into unconsciousness, stripped him, and set a fire under lamppost. (The mob was fond of burning Negroes while they lynched them.) They were on the point of lynching Alfred when, at the last possible moment, Frederick Merrick, a local grocer, showed up with a band of Germans and ordered the rioters to desist. The thugs threatened to hang Merrick as well, but he stood tall, pulled out his pistol, and invited the criminals to fight. They left to, as their leader said, clear out "another nest of niggers."

Mrs. Derrickson was carried to the hospital, where she died of her injuries the following month.[65]

Other African Americans were not so fortunate. One three year old boy was tossed out of a window to his death. Among the children who were murdered was a nephew of Robert John Simmons, a first sergeant in the 54th Massachusetts Infantry Regiment, whose family home was destroyed by the mob. Simmons probably never knew it. He was killed in action in the Battle of Fort Wagner, South Carolina, on July 18.[66]

At 11:45 p.m., Police Central received a report that sharp fighting was in progress in the 5th Precinct and had been for some time. The 5th was reinforced by the military. (No record of which unit has been found.) It held its positions.

At the same time, 20th Precinct reported the mob drove African Americans out of their houses on 36th Street near 7th Avenue. Some of them were murdered. No private homes dared take them in for fear of the mob. Those who could fled to the 20th for shelter, but it was full. The captain sent them to 16th Precinct.

Meanwhile, the 9th New York National Guard Regiment and the 83rd New York Volunteers (both two-year units now out of Federal service) reconstituted themselves and joined the fighting. There were also minor disturbances in

---

65 Barnet Schecter, *The Devil's Own Work* (New York: 2005), pp. 196-97; Iver Bernstein, *The New York City Draft Riots* (New York and Oxford: 1990), pp. 30-31.

66 Schecter, p. 242. One source stated that Simmons was mortally wounded on July 18 but did not succumb to his wounds until August.

Brooklyn along the East River waterfront, but it did not amount to much. (Some grain elevators were burned by disgruntled laborers on Thursday, but there was no general rioting.) The criminal element in Brooklyn understood the best opportunity for plunder was in Manhattan.

As July 14 merged into July 15, large parts of the city below 40th Street were completely in the hands of the mob.

CHAPTER VIII
WEDNESDAY: THE THIRD DAY

As the riot entered into its third day, Police Central at 300 Mulberry Street was a beehive of activity. The basement was the communications center, with wires going all over the city. It was also the supply center, filled with food taken from local grocery stores. The first floor was occupied by Acton, Brown, and a host of staff officers, inspectors, police captains, detectives, and patrolmen. The second floor was the domain of clerks and bureaucrats. The top floor was crowded with refugees, most of whom were African Americans.

Just after midnight, the 5th Precinct reported the mob was about to attack its station house because they were sheltering Negroes. Fortunately for them, the military arrived just in time and dispersed the rioters.

There was fighting on Grand Street shortly after midnight. Storekeepers fired on the mob to defend their property. At 12:20 a.m., Police President Acton signaled 13th Precinct he was sending a force to Grand Street. At the same time, the 21st Precinct reported a building on fire at the corner of 2nd Avenue and 33rd Street. The 15th Precinct sent reinforcements without consulting Police Central but informed them later. Acton also sent reinforcements.

At 12:30 a.m., the mob was destroying the African American church on 30th Street between 7th and 8th Avenues. They were attacked and dispersed by men from the 20th Precinct. Twenty minutes later, the 26th Precinct informed Police Central the government store on Greenwich Street was on fire. About the same time, a spy returned from 11th Precinct and announced a number of bands of robbers, each totaling 50 to 100 men, were breaking into stores on Houston Street near Attorney Street. Another spy reported the mob cleared out of the 21st Precinct station house. Even so, Thomas Acton sent a message to the newspapers, stating the police controlled the city. This dispatch was obviously premature.

The city was relatively quiet from about 1 a.m. to 6 a.m. A leader of the mob conveyed word to the newspaper editors: "The mob has control of the city, and is about to have more of it."[67]

When Wednesday, July 15, dawned, it was sultry. It would be the hottest day of the year. Only one street car line was working and that was on 6th Avenue. By early morning, there were thousands of marauders in the streets. Most businesses were closed, except the 5,000 liquor stores within the riot area, which did a great business.

At 7 a.m., the 29th Precinct signaled that African Americans were being forced out of their homes on 32nd Street. Many of them were already at the station house, although it was virtually undefended. There were only two police employees there—the telegraph operator and the doorman. Police Central signaled back and asked if there were any trouble, but at that moment, the line was cut.

Service was restored at 7:20 a.m. The 29th signaled that a Negro was hanging from a tree on 32nd Street. "Send us aid immediately," they telegraphed.[68] General Brown sent them Lieutenant Colonel Thaddeus Mott of the 14th New York Cavalry with a company of volunteers and an artillery battery from the 8th New York under Captain John H. Howell.[69]

It was 9 a.m. before Colonel Mott arrived at 32nd Street and 8th Avenue, where he spotted three hanging Negroes who had been lynched. The mob was now partying and dancing underneath them in celebration. Mott, who was on horseback, immediately drew his sword, rode into the crowd, and cut down one of the African Americans. This infuriated the horde, which attacked the infantry with rocks and pavement stones. One of the thugs tried to pull the colonel off his horse, so Mott ran him through. Meanwhile, the foot soldiers fixed bayonets.

Captain Howell stepped in front of his guns and ordered the crowd to disperse. He obviously did not want to fire on them. Mistaking compassion for weakness, the mob surged forward, trying to capture the guns. Perhaps they

---

67 Stoddard, p. 216.

68 Stoddard, p. 225.

69 Colonel Thaddeus Mott was a soldier of fortune. Born in New York City in 1831, he was a natural linguist. At age 17, he left for revolutionary Italy and earned a commission under Giuseppe Garibaldi. Then he turned sailor and served on various chipper ships; served in the Mexican Army during the Reform War; and joined the Union Army as a captain of artillery. He rose rapidly and was named lieutenant colonel and commander of the 14th New York Cavalry in 1863.

Colonel Thaddeus Mott

Colonel Cleveland Winslow

Regimental commanders during the Draft Riots. Mott is in the uniform of an Egyptian general, circa 1871.

thought the howitzers were loaded with blank shells or Howell was bluffing. The captain, however, was not bluffing, and his guns were loaded with grape and canister. He fired into the throng at almost point-blank range, littering the pavement for two blocks with dead, dying, and wounded. He continued to fire until the entire mob ran away. At least 25 people were killed outright. Several of the dead were women. Dozens of other people were wounded and, without proper medical care, several of them almost certainly died later.

In the meantime, about 7:30 a.m., the 20th Precinct reported the mob was hanging African Americans. The soldiers were previously there but were ordered downtown and left. Now they came back, but the precinct had only 100 policemen and asked for help.[70]

At 7:45 a.m., the 15th Precinct reported the streetcars on 6th Avenue were no longer running. There were few potential passengers in any event.

Throughout the morning, disturbances were reported from precinct after precinct. The telegraph services were interrupted many times. Dispatches and orders were being delivered by runners, which was a risky business for the messengers.

Meanwhile, a mob of about 1,000 sacked a large dry-goods business on Avenue C, and more than $40,000 worth of property was gobbled up. This amounted to almost a million dollars in 2018 money.

At 9 a.m., the 27th Precinct telegraphed that the mob was going to loot the building on the corner of Greenwich and Albany Streets. (Apparently, they got this information from spies.) The 26th Precinct sent a large force to intercept them and saved the business.

Black people continued to be targets. At 7 a.m. on July 15, a western New York City mob captured a Negro and hanged him at the corner of 7th Avenue and 29th Street. At midday, another African American man was hanged near the same location. On 27th Street that same morning, an African American was dragged out of his home, beaten, and hanged.

The police were short-handed everywhere. At 11:15 a.m., Acton ordered 16th Precinct to allow citizens to take charge of its station house and hold it against the mob, thus freeing the police for other duties.

---

70 Apparently this number included "Specials."

Meanwhile, a detachment of infantry under Captain Franklin S. Reynolds was attacked and surrounded on 1st Avenue. It escaped annihilation only by firing rapidly and engaging in hand-to-hand combat. Between 30 and 40 rioters were killed and many more were wounded. The soldiers also suffered casualties.

Acton ordered the 11th Precinct to reinforce the gas-house on 14th Street that morning. It provided gas light service to a large area and was the target of the mob. Acton was determined to keep the city's lights on.

* * *

At noon, the City Board of Aldermen met, and with the concurrence of the Board of Councilmen, they appropriated $2,500,000 to pay "exemption money" for drafted men who could not pay it themselves. This amounted to about the same sum as the city later paid for the buildings which the mob burned during the riots. In doing so, the aldermen removed the cause for the riot. No Irish immigrant or any other resident of New York City would be forced to fight in Mr. Lincoln's War if he did not want to. Although no one wanted to admit it, the rioters won. The situation was now analogous to a pot of boiling water. One can turn the fire off, but the pot does not stop boiling instantly. It will take some time to cool. This was certainly the case with the mob. It also took some time for word of the appropriation to reach the marauders.

* * *

Dispatches continued to pour into or out of Police Central Wednesday afternoon. They included the following:

(A little after noon): 13th Precinct reported things were "lively; storekeepers have fired into the mob" protecting their own property.

(12:20 p.m.): from 21st Precinct: building at the corner of 33rd Street and 2nd Avenue set on fire.

(12:50): from 15th Precinct: sent assistance to 21st Precinct.

(12:55): from 26th Precinct: Government stores in Greenwick are on fire.

(1:10 pm.): from 27th Precinct: send reinforcements immediately.

(1:25): from 4th Precinct: fire at the corner of Catherine Street and East Broadway.

(1:45): 11th Precinct reports several bands of robbers, each of 50 to 100 men, breaking into stores on Houston, near Attorney Street.

(1:47): from 29th Precinct: mob has cleared the 21st Precinct station house.

(2:00): from 29th Precinct: large mob surrounded Captain Green's house on 28th Street and 3rd Avenue. They threatened to hang him. He escaped out the back window.

(3:10): to 11th Precinct: send military to foot of 14th Street at East River.

(3:25): from 20th Precinct: mob sacking houses at 27th Street and 7th Avenue. "We have no force to send."

(3:30): from 21st Precinct: "colored people" in 2nd Avenue between 28th and 29th Streets being attacked.

(3:40): from 11th Precinct: send help to 242 Stanton Street and take possession of 5,000 cavalry swords stored there.

(3:55): 21st Precinct reports large crowd in 35th Street near 3rd Avenue. No assistance provided by adjoining precincts.

(4:43): from 20th Precinct: mob about to attack the 22nd Precinct station house.

(5:15): from 16th Precinct: send 100 shields and clubs for Specials.

(5:15): from 29th Precinct: who feeds the Specials? ANSWER: you do. REPLY: no money. ANSWER: that makes no difference.

(5:20): from 29th Precinct: rioters have just killed a Negro and are now on 28th Street and 7th Avenue. They have pickaxes and crowbars and intend to cut off the gas.[71]

(5:25 p.m.): from 1st Precinct: Riot at Pier 4, North River. The mob has killed Negroes there.[72]

---

71 The military arrived in time to prevent this.

72 All dispatches are from Headley, pp. 235-37.

In the middle all of this, General Sandford sent word that he had so many African Americans at the arsenal, he had to get rid of them. Police President Acton replied: "Tell General Sandford he must do the best he can with them there."[73]

At 12:25 p.m., Captain John Helme of the 27th Precinct signaled Police Central that he just learned there were 20,000 muskets stored in two bonded warehouses on Greenwich Street, and the mob was trying to seize them.

Had the mob attempted to take the warehouses earlier in the morning, they would have been successful, but now they failed. Had these warehouses been attacked on July 13, it would have been a disaster for the city—even if the mob lacked ammunition and only used bayonets on the muskets. Now, however, the attack failed.

At 2 p.m., Police Central received word that a large number of muskets were stored in a building on Broadway near 33rd Street. General Brown ordered Colonel Meyer to go there with 33 men from Hawkins' Zoaves and take possession of them. He waded through the mob and seized the arms. At that moment, an Irishman was passing by with his cart. Meyer appropriated the cart, dumped the muskets into it, and departed.

The mob continued to vent its fury throughout the day, although its intensity seemed less in the afternoon. No doubt the alcohol and the heat had something to do with that.

But the mob's hatred for people of color remained undiminished. At 3:15 p.m., the 29th Precinct reported the mob was burning buildings on 2nd Avenue near 28th Street. Some of the houses here were occupied by African Americans, who were running for their lives. Ten minutes later, the 20th Precinct reported that the mob was sacking houses in the vicinity of 27th Street and 7th Avenue. It had no police to send there.

The clashes were now bloodier than earlier. The response by the authorities was also much more rapid. "But [only] a small proportion of the casualties were ever formally reported . ..", Stoddard wrote later.[74]

That afternoon, the mob was clearly concentrating against the telegraph lines. The police repairmen could not keep up, although the police telegraph system was never completely incapacitated.

---

73 Headley, p. 237.

74 Stoddard, p. 234.

For a time, trouble seemed to focus on the 21st Precinct, which reported that the situation there was very bad. A large crowd was forming in 35th Street near 3rd Avenue. The 21st called for help at 3:50 p.m. Five minutes later, it signaled that the mob had captured five or six African Americans and was preparing to hang them. Help arrived from Police Central—but too late.

Overall, however, the authorities felt the tide turned—as indeed it did. Just after 4 p.m., the gas-house at the foot of 14th Street reported it had 84 regular army soldiers—enough to ensure lighting for much of the city that night. Fifteen minutes later, 16th Precinct requested 100 special shields and clubs to arm citizen volunteers, who were assembling rapidly. The rioters were not yet ready to call it quits, however. At 5:20 p.m., Captain Francis C. Speight of the 29th Precinct reported the insurgents were now at 7th Avenue and 28th Street, where they had just killed an African American. They carried pick-axes and crowbars and were planning to cut off the gas. They were also about to burn some buildings in the area.

This time, Acton had nothing to send them. He signaled back that Speight would have to do the best he could with the men he had. Fortunately, at just the right time, soldiers arrived with rifles and bayonets. The mob ran. A few houses on 28th Street between 1st and 2nd Avenues were on fire, but that was all.

The 65th New York National Guard Regiment under Lieutenant Colonel William Berens boarded railroad cars in Pennsylvania at 4 a.m. and arrived in the city about 5 p.m.[75] It had a battery of four howitzers from 8th New York National Guard attached. As it marched away from the docks, a mob formed and attempted to take two cooks from the 8th Artillery, no doubt intending to lynch them. The Guardsmen would not allow it. Berens reported to General Wool, who ordered him to report to General Brown, who directed him to send two companies to guard the treasury buildings on Wall Street. Two other companies were used to restore order on Union Square. The rest of the 65th bivouacked nearby.

About 5 p.m., General Sandford bestirred himself and sent 150 infantrymen and two rifled cannons under Colonel Sherwood to suppress a mob at the corner of 27th Street and 7th Avenue. When the troops arrived, flames were bursting out of the windows of the building and a black man was dangling from a lamppost. At that moment, a fire engine arrived from the other direction. Part of the crowd

---

75 Lieutenant Colonel William Berens was born in Hanover, Lower Saxony (Niedersachsen), Germany, in 1826. When the War for Southern Independence began, he was appointed major, 5th Wisconsin Infantry Regiment, then lieutenant colonel of the 65th New York. Later he was named colonel of the 187th New York, but this regiment was never mustered in because of a lack of volunteers.

took shelter behind the firemen. The soldiers backed off, leaving the field in the possession of the insurgents, and returned to the armory. The mob then hanged two more Negroes.

At 5:25 p.m., a telegram arrived at Police Central, stating there was a riot at Pier 4 on the North River. Several Negroes were killed.

A message arrived at 6:40 p.m. from Captain Alanson S. Wilson of the 32nd Precinct, who reported the residents were leaving Carmansville and Fort Washington (at the upper end of the island) because they thought the mob would be there that night. He wanted to withdraw. Acton approved.

Wilson was concerned about a possible mob raid into the upper part of West Manhattan Island. It was sparsely populated by wealthy people. There were no soldiers here and only a few policemen. There were also plenty of Negro domestic servants there who could be tortured and hanged. Fortunately, the mob was running out of gas, to use a 21st Century expression. The suspected attack did not materialize.

The night of July 15/16 gave the mobs and gangs one last chance for robbery and pillage. Under the cover of darkness, fires and break-ins occurred everywhere. "There were increasing indications that some of the more densely ignorant of the lower classes of recent immigration had got it into their dull brains that this was a 'revolution' of some sort," William O. Stoddard recalled.[76] Not realizing the strength of the mob was waning because the cause of the riot had been removed, they chose another ambitious target.

The USS Dunderberg was under construction at Webb's shipyard. The workers, who had contacts in the mob, warned the military commanders that the rioters intended to capture and burn this ironclad. Members of the 7th New York Militia Regiment and the 22nd New York Militia Regiment organized at the 7th Regiment Armory and marched to protect it.

A little before 9 p.m., about 400 veterans under Major Nevers arrived just as 1,000 rioters did. They were headed for the ship. When the soldiers lowered their bayonets for a charge, the mob fled. The troops remained around the Dunderberg until daylight.

---

76 Stoddard, p. 244.

Meanwhile, about 6 p.m., another mob gathered at 1st Avenue between 18th and 19th Streets. General Sandford ordered Colonel Cleveland Winslow to clear it out.[77] He took an ad hoc force of 150 men and a couple of howitzers, which were being directed by Colonel Edward E. Jardine.[78]

Jardine was a veteran. Born in Brooklyn in 1828, he grew up in poverty. Nevertheless, he became a successful hardware importer. He joined the New York National Guard, became part of the Union Army in May 1861, and eventually earned a commission in the 9th New York. He fought at Big Bethel, in the Hatteras Expedition, and in North Carolina, before returning to Virginia in 1862. There, he fought at South Mountain, Antietam, and Fredericksburg, and he was wounded twice. In the process, he rose to the rank of major. When the regiment's term of enlistment expired in 1863, it returned to New York City and was mustered out on May 20. Governor Seymour, however, promoted Jardine to colonel on May 29 and ordered him to reform the unit for three years' service as the 9th New York Veteran Volunteer Infantry Regiment. Most of the men, however, did not reenlist.

Winslow engaged the rioters at 1st Avenue and 19th Streets and was supported by Major Robison and Duryea's Zouaves, as well as two howitzers. Badly outnumbered, the soldiers were defeated by the mob. Colonel Jardine was severely wounded by a sniper who specialized in shooting officers. A slug struck Jardine in the thigh. He and two other wounded officers were rescued by two young women (local residents) who held no sympathy for the thugs and hid him in their basement. The outlaws found him anyway. Fortunately for the colonel, one of the rioters was a friend of his. He stood over Jardine and would not let his

---

77 Cleveland Winslow was born in Medford, Massachusetts, on May 26, 1836. He enlisted in the 5th New York (Duryea's Zouaves) when the war began and was soon promoted to captain and company commander. He served with this regiment in the Seven Days campaign, Second Manassas, and Antietam, and was promoted to colonel on December 4, 1862. Winslow was a disciplinarian and unpopular with his men.

78 The 5th New York (Duryea's Zouaves) was mustered out when its two-year enlistment expired after the Battle of Chancellorsville. It was reconstituted for the New York Draft Riots. Like all such regiments, it was severely understrength, amounting to a weak battalion.

comrades in disorder touch him. They beat the other wounded officers to death. Perhaps to protect him, Jardine never revealed the name of his benefactor or why the man saved his life.[79]

Colonel Winslow marched into an ambush. The mob threw rocks from roofs and fired pistols and muskets. The fire was in volleys, as if it was organized. The gunners fired 10 rounds of grape and canister into the crowd, and the slaughter was horrendous. The ground was cleared, and there were rows of bodies for two blocks, but that did nothing to mitigate the fire from the houses, which grew hotter. Winslow ordered his troops to retire. They suffered 10% casualties, excluding minor injuries.

At 11 p.m., another force of 150 men and two guns under Captains Putnam and Shelby arrived. They fired grape and canister into the crowd and swept 1st Avenue clear. The troops remained until 12:30 a.m. on Thursday, July 16.

In the meantime, rioters expended their wrath on African Americans. At around 7 p.m., they seized yet another man, beat him, hanged him from a tree, sliced him with knives, and as Stoddard wrote, "torturing him to death with the ingenuity of so many Apache red men."[80] When the police recovered the body, they found all his fingers and toes were chopped off.

There were a great many fires during the night of July 15/16, but overall, New York City was lucky. There was no wind.

It was now obvious to many that the mob's hold on the city was weakening. There were no assaults on well-defended positions. Authorities were in control of the city above 42nd Street. But the rampagers were still dangerous. At 10:05 p.m., they surrounded the African American quarters from Sullivan Street to Thompson Street. Several dwellings were burned. Attacks on brothels were also prominent that night.

Sometime between 10 p.m. and midnight, another significant event occurred. The Jersey City ferryboat docked at the Canal Street landing. Out stepped Lieutenant Colonel Thomas Holt's veteran 74th New York Infantry Regiment.[81] A

---

79 Jardine never fully recovered from his wounds. He briefly commanded the 17th New York Infantry Regiment (newly formed from the 7th and 9th New York Regiments) but was physically not up to the demands of this position, and he transferred to the Veteran Reserve Corps. He was breveted brigadier general and discharged in May 1865. He went into business after the war and became an editor and publisher of the Jersey City Daily Times.

80 Stoddard, p. 247,

81 The 74th New York was also known as the 5th Excelsior Regiment.

former National Guard unit, it became part of the Union Army in 1861 and had previously fought in the Peninsula Campaign (including the Siege of Yorktown, the Battle of Williamsburg, and the Seven Days' Campaign), Second Manassas, Fredericksburg, Chancellorsville, and most recently Gettysburg, where it had suffered heavy casualties. They were a colorful lot, with uniforms (depending on the company) patterned after the French chasseurs (light infantry) or Zouaves, which featured a dark blue jacket with yellow trimming, a dark blue vest with yellow trim, a sky blue sash, a red fez cap with a yellow tassel, bright red pantaloons with yellow trim, and white gaiters (protective clothing for the ankles and legs below the knee). Despite their French appearance, most of the troops were German-Americans from New York City.

CHAPTER IX
THE FOURTH DAY

On the fourth day of rioting, the water that was boiling on Monday and Tuesday began to cool, and the force of the riot was clearly diminishing. Word spread that no one would have to serve in the Union Army if they didn't want to, which deprived the mob of its strength. The appearance of regular Federal infantry regiments also cooled the ardor of many would-be marauders as well. Some die-hard rioters, however, still existed: idealist young men who wanted a true workers' revolution, and thugs who just wanted the crime spree to continue.

On the other side, troops continued to pour into the city. At 4 a.m., even before the sun rose, the 28th Precinct reported that the 7th New York Infantry Regiment landed near Canal Street and was marching to Broadway and then to Police Central.[82] It was a reconstituted unit. Formed in April 1861, less than two weeks after Fort Sumter, it fought at Big Bethel, in the Peninsula Campaign, the Seven Days, Sharpsburg (Antietam), Fredericksburg, and Chancellorsville. It was consolidated with the remnants of the 52nd New York Infantry Regiment on May 8, 1863, was redesignated 7th New York Veteran Infantry Regiment, and fought at Gettysburg.

That morning, the city instructed the streetcar companies to resume normal operations. This order was premature. Around 8:35 a.m., the mob stopped a streetcar at 2nd Avenue and 23rd and made it turn back. The street car drivers wisely suspended further operations.

Violence against people of color continued. Around 7 a.m., a mob of 50 men attacked a black man, chased him to the 34th Street ferry, beat him, threw him from the dock and drowned him.

---

82 This 7th New York Volunteer Infantry is not to be confused with the 7th New York National Guard (Militia), which was another regiment altogether. Both fought in the Draft Riots.

Meanwhile, at 10 a.m., another veteran infantry regiment from the veteran Excelsior Brigade arrived. They paraded through some of the areas where the rioting was the worst. No one raised a hand against them.

In other districts which were considered less dangerous, patrols were conducted by armed members of the Citizens' Volunteer Police Reserves. This took pressure off the overworked and nearly exhausted regular police.

Another turning point occurred when Catholic Archbishop John Hughes finally issued a strong verbal plea to stop the rioting. Mayor Opdyke called upon him to make such an entreaty as early as Monday. The prelate issued a lukewarm appeal for peace on Tuesday (which was published on Wednesday), but it didn't amount to much. Why he waited until now to issue a strong appeal is not known. A written version of Hughes' more forceful plea was published in the newspapers on Thursday and also appeared as a poster. By noon, all the Catholics in the mob knew the bishop strongly condemned what they were doing.

There was still fear. The Delamater Iron Works refused to resume operations without police and/or military protection, but it was a quieter day overall.

That morning, authorities felt confident enough in the improving situation to start addressing the refugee problem. They started with the former residents of the Colored Orphan Asylum, who were sleeping in police station houses or at the overcrowded City Orphanage on Bloomingdale Road (in upper Manhattan) since Monday. They were escorted by 50 policemen because the city leaders were still not sure how safe the streets were. The black children were transported to the Battery, put aboard a steamer, and sent to the City Hospital on Blackwell's Island, where adequate quarters were available.

Probably the worse incident of the day began around 8 a.m. A large crowd assembled near Gramercy Park, at 2nd Avenue and 22nd Street. A squadron of dismounted horsemen and some city militia, led by Colonel Mott, attempted to disperse a mob on 3rd Avenue near 21st Street. The rioters fired from the roofs, and the soldiers were soon in a critical position. They retreated in disorder; then they broke and ran. The mob pursued them for several blocks. About 25 of them took shelter in Jackson Foundry, where they were penned down.

The order committing Mott's force came from General Wool or General Sandford—it was never made clear which. In any case, no one saw fit to inform Commissioner Acton or General Brown. The colonel went to Police Central and asked for help. Here he was reprimanded by Brown and told to return to his men.

Brown sent a relief column under Captain Putnam—who was about to receive a special promotion to major—to the site of the disaster, accompanied by his men. He found the street deserted by both parties. He pushed on to 3rd Avenue near 20th Street, where he found his way blocked by the mob. Suddenly, the crowd attacked. Heavy skirmishing continued for some time. Putnam responded by turning his cannons on the rioters and giving them "a whiff of grape." He later reported 13 rioters killed and 24 wounded. The soldiers in the foundry were not rescued until 3 p.m.

This engagement, sometimes called the Battle of Gramercy Park, was the last major action of the New York Draft Riots.

Between midnight on July 16 and sunrise on Friday, July 17, the riot finally played out.

On the morning of July 17, the police prepared to arrest known rioters. The cops, however, were still not able to walk down the street alone and in uniform. They patrolled the streets in groups of six.

That same morning, Secretary of War Stanton sacked General Brown, for reasons which were never made clear. He was replaced by Brigadier General E. R. S. Canby. The next day, John E. Wool was relieved and, like Brown, sent into involuntary retirement. He was succeeded as commander of the Department of the East by Major General John A. Dix, a former U.S. senator from New York and a former Secretary of the Treasury. He was also a Democrat.

EPILOGUE
THE COSTS

Esteemed historian Samuel Eliot Morison called the New York Draft Riots the "equivalent to a Confederate victory."[83] If so, it was the strangest Confederate victory of the war because there was not an armed Rebel within 100 miles of the place. But, when I look at the roster of military units sent to the city and away from Robert E. Lee and his men, I have to agree with Dr. Morison. Most historians say that five regiments were diverted to the city, and they cite a dispatch Secretary of War Edwin Stanton sent to Governor Seymour immediately after the Battle of Gettysburg. It is true that Stanton ordered five regiments to head for the city—*initially*. It is also true that he quickly dispatched several others. The following is a partial list of regiments in the Big Apple as of Friday morning, July 17, 1863. All are infantry regiments unless otherwise noted:

5th New York

7th New York National Guard

7th New York (the "Old Guard")

8th New York National Guard

9th New York "Hawkins Zouaves"

10th New York National Guard

10th New York

11th New York

13th New York Cavalry (from Rochester)

---

83 Samuel Eliot Morison, *The Oxford History of the American People* (New York: 1972), Volume II, p. 451.

14th New York Cavalry

17th New York

22nd New York National Guard

26th Michigan

47th New York National Guard

52nd New York

54th New York

65th New York National Guard

69th New York National Guard

74th New York National Guard

83rd New York

152nd New York

This list does not include 700 sailors and Marines committed to the action, or 150 regular infantry provided daily from the garrisons and fortifications in the harbor. It also does not include several temporarily reconstituted regiments which were recently mustered out of service, including the 1st New York; the 4th New York; the 12th Heavy Artillery; the 17th Chasseurs; the 31st New York; the 37th New York; the 38th New York; and others. Although they were veteran units and formidable foes, none of these regiments were at anything close to full strength.

* * *

How many people were killed or injured in the riots?

Exact statistics on casualties in the riots do not exist. The War Department didn't even release its casualty figures, which suggests they were pretty high. One prominent historian placed the number of dead of all parties (rioters, police, and military) at 119 or 120, more than half of whom were blacks. This number, in my humble opinion, is ridiculously low. If more than half of those killed were African American, which means 59 was the maximum number of rioters, soldiers, policemen, etc., who were killed. And yet, people were firing into the mob with cannons, Gatling guns, muskets, and rifles, not to mention the police, who broke skulls with their heavy locust clubs, tossed rock throwers off buildings, or shot them with their revolvers. Both soldiers and Marines also fought the rioters at close quarters with fixed bayonets. After reading this book, I don't see how a reader can conclude that there were only 120 or so fatalities.

One authority on the gangs of New York estimated 2,000 people were killed and about 8,000 were injured.[84] This estimate seems high. Police President Acton stated that about 1,200 were killed.[85] New York City police estimated that 1,200 to 1,500 rioters were killed.[86] One military authority estimated it at 1,300.[87] Superintendent Kennedy said 1,159 people were killed, exclusive of those who were secretly buried.[88] A detective at the War Department placed the death toll at 1,462.[89] "On the part of police and military the mortuary records are almost equally scanty," William O. Stoddard recorded. Burial permits were not issued for many of the dead, as the city's bureaucracy temporarily ceased to operate for obvious reasons. Many of the Irish simply buried their dead in a vacant lot or in a tenement cellar without bothering to apply for official permission. They could not have afforded to purchase a cemetery plot or pay a fee for a burial permit in any case. "There were many killed and wounded, and no more can be said," Stoddard wrote.[90] James Howell Street also declared that the exact number killed is unknown.[91] In addition, about 3,000 African Americans were left homeless by the riots. Many left the city, never to return. The African American population dropped to its lowest level since 1820.

If 120 people were killed and more than half of them were black, then at least 61 blacks were killed (or murdered) in the riots. Again, documentation is lacking, but I have seen estimates of more than 200. I suspect that, if less than 200 African Americans were killed, the total did not fall short of that by much. Many of them were lynched. Taken as a whole, the New York Draft Riots were the largest mass murdering of members of an ethnic group in U.S. history.

---

84 Herbert Asbury, *The Gangs of New York* (New York: 1928), p. 169.

85 McCague, p. 178.

86 Stoddard, p. 293.

87 Stoddard, p. 293.

88 Cook, p. 193.

89 *Ibid.*, p. 193.

90 Stoddard, pp. 293-94.

91 Street, pp. 88-89.

We do not know exactly how many of these people were hanged, but many of them were. The Draft Riots were also probably the largest mass lynching in U.S. history.[92]

Property damage was estimated at $5,000,000, or roughly one billion dollars in today's currency. No estimate of the cost of lost wages, lost production time, or lost jobs was ever made, but it was huge.

Generally speaking, the rioters got off light. Only one of them was tried in Federal District Court. His name was John U. Andrews, a lawyer from Virginia, who encouraged the mob to riot in front of the draft office on July 13 and who led it in cheers for Jefferson Davis. He was found guilty of treason, engaging in rebellion against the United States, conspiracy, and aiding and resisting the draft. His sentence was three years at hard labor.[93]

The city arrested 443 suspected rioters but 221 were released without any charges filed against them. The grand jury did not indict 36 of the others, and several more jumped bail and disappeared. In the end, only 65 were convicted in the Court of General Sessions or the Court of Special Sessions. Most of them pled guilty in some sort of plea bargaining arrangement. Only 13 were actually tried. The shiftiest sentence was six months in the City Penitentiary.[94]

One rioter was indicted for murdering Ann Derrickson, a white woman married to a black man. He pled guilty in State Court to a lesser charge and received two years in Sing Sing. A woman also got two years' imprisonment for stealing 120 pairs of gloves. One thug was indicted for two counts of first-degree robbery but pled guilty to one charge of assault and battery. He was fined six cents. Only one man received a heavy sentence for attacking or murdering Negroes: Joseph Marshall was given 10 years in state prison.[95]

---

92 Lynchings and hangings are two different things. Hangings can be legal executions. Lynchings involve killing someone who has not been found guilty of a crime at a legal trial, usually using a rope.

93 Cook, pp. 184-87.

94 *Ibid.,* pp, 178-79.

95 Schecter, p. 258; Cook, pp. 179-80.

BIBLIOGRAPHY

Asbury, Herbert. *The Gangs of New York*. New York: 1928.

Bernstein, Iver. *The New York City Draft Riots*. New York and Oxford: 1990.

Brummer, Sidney D. *Political History of New York State During the Period of the Civil War*. Wahroonga, New South Wales: 2015.

Charles River Editors. *The New York City Draft Riots of 1863*. Columbia, SC: 2016.

Cook, Adrian. *The Armies of the Streets: The New York City Draft Riots of 1863*. Lexington, Kentucky: 1974.

Ewing, E. W. R. *Northern Rebellion and Southern Secession*. Richmond, Virginia: 1904.

Fremantle, Arthur. *Three Months in the Southern States*. New York: 1864.

Harris, Leslie M. *In the Shadow of Slavery: African Americans in New York City, 1626-1863*. Chicago: 2003.

Headley, Joel Tyler. *The Great Riots of New York*. New York: 1873.

Horsmanden, Daniel. "*The New York Conspiracy of 1741*" in the Gilder Institute of American History, https://gilderlehrman.org/content/new-york-conspiracy-1741. Accessed 2018.

BIBLIOGRAPHY

Hummel, Jeffrey R. *Emancipating Slaves, Enslaving Free Men*. Chicago: 1996.

Long, E. B. *The Civil War Day by Day*. Garden City, New York: 1971.

McCague, James. *The Second Rebellion: The Story of the New York City Draft Riots of 1863*.

McManus, Edgar J. *Black Bondage in the North*. Syracuse, New York: 1973.

McManus, Edgar J. *Emancipating Slaves, Enslaving Free Men*. Chicago: 1966.

Morison, Samuel Eliot. *The Oxford History of the American People*. New York: 1972. 2 Volumes.

Oltman, Adele. "*The Hidden History of Slavery in New York*." The Nation, November 7, 2005.

Schecter, Barnet. *The Devil's Own Work*. New York: 2005

"*Statistics on Slavery*." Faculty.weber.edu/kmackay/statistics_on_slavery.html.

Stoddard, William O. *Volcano Under the City*. New York: 1887.

Street, James Howell. *The Civil War*. New York: 1953.

"*Witchhunt in New York: The 1741 Rebellion*." https://pbs.org/wgbh/aia/part1/1p286.html. Accessed 2018.

ABOUT THE AUTHOR

Samuel W. Mitcham, Jr. is a former professor of military history and historical geography. He taught at Henderson State University, Georgia Southern University, and the University of Louisiana at Monroe. He is also a former visiting professor at the United States Military Academy. At the University of Louisiana at Monroe, he was named "My Favorite Professor" four times by the Baptist Student Association despite not being a Baptist. He was also named Freshman Honor Society's Professor of the Year.

He is the author of over 40 books including *Rommel's Desert War, Hitler's Legions, Why Hitler' The Genesis of the Third Reich, Vicksburg: The Bloody Siege that Turned the Tide of the Civil War, The Men of the Luftwaffe, Desert Fox: The Storied Career of Erwin Rommel*, and *Bust Hell Wide Open: The Life of Nathan Bedford Forrest, and It Wasn't About Slavery: Exposing the Great Lie of the Civil War (Forthcoming: January 2020).* In addition to writing books, he has also written dozens of articles and appeared on the History Channel, CBS, National Public Radio and the British Broadcasting Network. He is the former adviser to General Norman Schwarzkopf on the CBS Special *D-Day.*

He is the Holder of the Jefferson Davis Gold Medal for the Writing and Research of Southern History. Mitcham is also the former President and CEO of TelSon Communications, a private $7 million corporation that provided local exchange service in seven states. He attended Northeast Louisiana University, North Carolina State University and received his Ph.D. from the University of Tennessee. Mitcham is also a former U.S. Army helicopter pilot and company commander.

AVAILABLE FROM SHOTWELL PUBLISHING

If you enjoyed this book, perhaps some of our other titles will pique your interest. The following titles are now available for your reading pleasure... Enjoy!

Joyce Bennett

Maryland, My Maryland: The Cultural Cleansing of a Small Southern State

Jerry Brewer

Dismantling the Republic

Andrew P. Calhoun, Jr.

My Own Darling Wife: Letters From a Confederate Volunteer [John Francis Calhoun]

John Chodes

Segregation: Federal Policy or Racism?

Washington's KKK: The Union League During Southern Reconstruction

Paul C. Graham

Confederaphobia: An American Epidemic

When the Yankees Come: Former South Carolina Slaves Remember Sherman's Invasion

Joseph Jay

Sacred Conviction: The South's Stand for Biblical Authority

Suzanne Parfitt Johnson

Maxcy Gregg's Sporting Journal 1842 - 1858

James R. Kennedy

Dixie Rising: Rules for Rebels

James R. & Walter D. Kennedy

Punished with Poverty: The Suffering South

Yankee Empire: Aggressive Abroad and Despotic At Home

Philip Leigh

The Devil's Town: Hot Spring During the Gangster Era

U.S. Grant's Failed Presidency

Michael Martin

Southern Grit: Sensing the Siege at Petersburg

Lewis Liberman

Snowflake Buddies: ABCs for Leftism for Kids!

Charles T. Pace

Lincoln As He Was

Southern Independence. Why War?

James Rutledge Roesch

From Founding Fathers to Fire Eaters: The Constitutional Doctrine of States' Rights in the Old South

Kirkpatrick Sale

*Emancipation Hell: The
Tragedy Wrought By Lincoln's
Emancipation Proclamation*

Karen Stokes

*A Legion of Devils: Sherman
in South Carolina*

Carolina Love Letters

John Vinson

Southerner, Take Your Stand!

Howard Ray White

Understanding Creation and Evolution

Walter Kirk Wood

*Beyond Slavery: The Northern
Romantic Nationalist Origins
of America's Civil War*

Clyde N. Wilson

*Annals of the Stupid Party: Republicans
Before Trump (The Wilson Files 3)*

*Lies My Teacher Told Me: The
True History of the War for
Southern Independence*

*Nullification: Reclaiming Consent of
the Governed (The Wilson Files 2)*

*The Old South: 50 Essential Books
(Southern Reader's Guide I)*

*The War Between the States:
60 Essential Books (Southern
Reader's Guide II)*

*The Yankee Problem: An American
Dilemma (The Wilson Files 1)*

———————————

GREEN ALTAR BOOKS

(Literary Imprint)

Randall Ivey

*A New England Romance &
Other SOUTHERN Stories*

James Everett Kibler

Tiller (Clay Bank County, IV)

Karen Stokes

Belles: A Carolina Romance

Honor in the Dust

The Immortals

*The Soldier's Ghost: A
Tale of Charleston*

———————————

GOLD-BUG

(Mystery & Suspense Imprint)

Michael Andrew Grissom

Billie Jo

Brandi Perry

Splintered: A New Orleans Tale

Martin L. Wilson

To Jekyll and Hide

Free Book Offer

Sign-up for new release notifications and receive a **FREE** downloadable edition of *Lies My Teacher Told Me: The True History of the War for Southern Independence* by Dr. Clyde N. Wilson by visiting FreeLiesBook.com or by texting the word "Dixie" to 345345. You can always unsubscribe and keep the book, so you've got nothing to lose!

www.ingramcontent.com/pod-product-compliance
Lightning Source LLC
LaVergne TN
LVHW041201080426
835511LV00006B/701